VOICES OF TACOMA
A GATHERING OF POETS

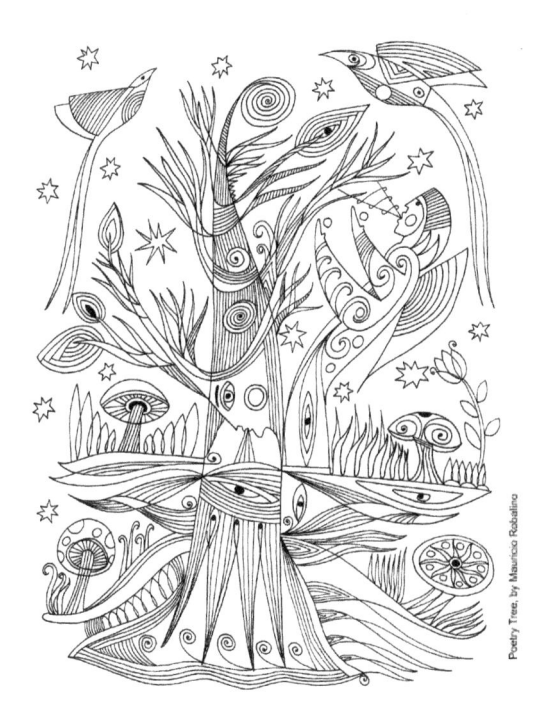

Poetry Tree, by Mauricio Robalino

Edited by Burl E. Battersby
Illustrated by Mauricio Robalino

Copyright © 2024 by Burl E. Battersby
Contributing authors and/or their original publishers retain all copyrights for individual poems.
Published by Be! Eugene Be! Creative in partnership with Blue Cactus Press.

All rights reserved. No part of this book may be reproduced or utilized in any form, or by any electronic, mechanical, or other means, without the prior written permission of the publisher.

Library of Congress Cataloging-in-Publication Data

Names: Burl E. Battersby, editor. | Mauricio Robalino, illustrator.
Title: Voices of Tacoma: A Gathering of Poets
Description: First edition. | Tacoma, WA. : Be! Eugene Be! Creative, 2024.
Identifiers: Library of Congress Control Number: 2024915663 | ISBN: 979-8-218-20817-2
Subjects: Pacific-Northwest Poetry; 21st Century American Poetry

This project was funded, in part, by the Tacoma Artists Initiative Program (2023-2024).

Be! Eugene Be! Creative
beeugenebecreative.com

1 2 3 4 5 6 7

INVOCATION
Omar Willey

I tell you, sisters, brothers
Kidder Mathews, Wright Runstad, and Goodman Real Estate
would have you believe that there is no history
here beyond their red lines, that
neighborhoods are not people but names
on Google Maps to be changed like
clothes with the stench of dirty money,
that the place where you now sit with us in gathering
exists within a void, separate from the past and future

This is not so

And so this day we remember
to honor,
remember to praise,
remember to love

All the earth cracked here
All the trees fell here
All the feet walked here
All the voices cried here
All the eyes wept here
All the souls released here
Their names are silent beneath your feet
as they etch into your bones

We thank you, elders, that this place of worship
still sings with us, and that we listen;
we thank you that this sacred ground still
connects us to our neighbors and our children;
we thank you that this lovely haven for the wayward
has not become a shopping mall.

Elders, spirits all,
You have borne the burden of our silence
and our ignorance;
tonight let us bear your hope.

From "Robert Lashley in conversation with Omar Willey" at King's Books, August 31, 2023
Creative Commons Attribution - ShareAlike 4.0 License. Share freely.

CONTENTS

INVOCATION	Omar Willey	iii
INTRODUCTION	Burl Battersby	x
Redlined	Frank D'Andrea	1
Tahoma Doesn't Love Us	Abby E. Murray	2
April	render jemis	3
At the Source of the Ore Our Smelter Processed	Elizabeth Bradfield	4
At St. Leo's	Katherine Van Eddy	5
Sonnenizio on Orchard Street	Micah Ackerman Hirsch	6
Red Elm Cafe on MLK Jr. Way	Andrea Clausen	7
Walking with the Birder at Wapato Park	Celeste Maria Schueler	8
November 3, 1885	Melody Derrick	9
It Feels Like	Liz Morrow	10
You Have an Accent	Jessica J. Bloodsaw	11
Today there is a breeze and nothing is on fire…	Michael Haeflinger	12
Elders Rage At Snake Lake After A Shootout	Robert Lashley	13
spearmint	Gloria Joy Kazuko Muhammad	14
red hood, white hood, blue hood	Albert de Santis	15
Charro 4 Charro	Vaquero Azul	16
Today's Tacoma	Andrea Clausen	17
Stopped and Frisked at University Place Suicide Blues	Robert Lashley	18
Where am I	B. Eugene B.	19
Witness	Josie Emmons Turner	20
Tacoma…	Beverly Mathews	21
The Otters of Chambers-Clover Creek	Claudia Riiff Finseth	22
Dear Ancestor	Christina Vega	23
After Tacoma | After Lewes	Micah Ackerman Hirsch	24
Rain	Abbie Hughes	25
Call It Futures	Micah Ackerman Hirsch	27
WHAT'S IN A NAME?	Anida Yoeu Ali	28
Surroundings	Roxann Murray	30
Squeeze	Katherine Van Eddy	31
Rain Cycle Centered	Maizy Apple Green	32
One Hundred Days of Solitude	Lucas Smiraldo	34
The Worm Moon	Tanner Abernathy	36
At the Goldfish Tavern	Kevin Miller	37
On Mount Rainier	Meredith Smith	38
Year's End Wright Park	Kevin Miller	39
All that is solid and melts must end up somewhere	William Kupinse	40
Eat My Food	Felicia Tran	42
Migration Song	Kristy Gledhill	43
Haiku of Destiny	Tia Pliskow	44
On the #1 Bus	Mary Bradford	45

She Comes to School	Josie Emmons Turner	46
Hold No Bitterness	Sandra K. King	47
Postscript in the Past Perfect	Allen Braden	48
Shakabrah Diner	Allen Braden	49
the mountain is bleeding out__	francis faye oak	50
SONNET IV - A Graduation Sonnet	Claudia Riiff Finseth	51
Tacomaturity	Trevor Neil White	52
an ode to the stadium district:	Isaac Rodriguez	56
The Way to Saint Pat	Emily Meyer	57
REFUGEE	N.L. Edwin	58
Tacoma Rainbow	Gertrude Haley Bader	60
Take a breath	Rebecca Amina Echeverria	61
Delinquent	Tammy Robacker	62
Beyond This Violet Fabric	Sandra K. King	64
Be Gay, Do Crime	Vaquero Azul	66
My Story Mixed	Jack Morrow	67
at the point of defiance__	francis faye oak	68
Nothing & Everything	Julie Van	69
Long Live the Kingdom of Front Yardia	Chloe Mohs	70
in Tacoma	Sarah Heavin	72
Hilltop Musings	Joshua Olver	74
Sequoia in the City	Phil Harty	75
Learn.	Xandra Egge	76
Away from Home	Felicia Tran	77
KIA Boys are loose	Thomas Nolan	78
Dawn in Tacoma	Tia Pliskow	79
What's the Destiny of the City of Destiny?	Allen Braden	80
The Point Obscured	Emily Meyer	81
Icarus in transit	Albert de Santis	82
Zooming Through	David Gilmour	83
you'll love, tacoma__	francis faye oak	84
S 74th to N 33rd on the Tree Street	Erik Hanberg	85
ii	Yuri Arakaki	87
Douche Bag	Sam Cori	88
one account of provenance-1	John Sexton	90
Propitious	Jessika Satori	91
Breakfast Burrito	B. Eugene B.	92
The Hilltop Heartbreak	Karen Cruz	94
Suspension	Melody Derrick	97
Liquid Dream's	Susan Harmon	98
The Donna of Destiny	Jessica J. Bloodsaw	100
What sounds like rain	Meredith Smith	102
Migrant's Vade Mecum	Kristy Gledhill	103
Sidewalk Poetry	Jessica Stovall	105
City of Destiny, City of Shame	Jacque Lynn Schultz	106

Poem in Which the Limits of a Gift Are Identified	Abby E. Murray	108
Outside Marcia's Silver Spoon	Albert de Santis	110
In the beginning	Alexa Hoggatt	112
Ivan	John Lawrence	114
You Can Go Anywhere	John Kulm	115
Swan Creek	Michael Haeflinger	116
Middle School Seminar	Rebecca Amina Echeverria	117
Ode to Autumn	Abbie Hughes	118
Sentipensante of Tacoma	Bailey Lonergan	119
6th is first	Jean-Pierre Garcia	120
First Snow in Tacoma: A Timeline	Chloe Mohs	121
TACOMA THEN/TACOMA NOW	Chelsea Eng	122
I See a Valley	Elaine Briden	127
Ode to a Gulch	Annelise Rue-Johns	128
Davit	Elizabeth Bradfield	129
+0.01	Abby E. Murray	130
First Date	Isaac Rodriguez	131
Self/Portrait of Tacoma	Liz Morrow	132
Holy Week	Tanner Abernathy	133
RIGHT ON, TACOMA! WRITE ON . . .	Dawn Ellis	134
Owen Beach: Antidote for Nonsense	Jessika Satori	138
The Mountain	Riley Egge	139
When A Child Tells The Tale	Jacqueline Ware	140
S. Tacoma Way (Surfaced)	Hannah Thornton	143
Wright Park Conservatory	Roger Iverson	144
Inpatient	Peter Jung	145
Implication	William Kupinse	146
Tacoma Flora	Clover Tamayo	147
Solo Point	Carl Papa Palmer	148
The Buddha of Pacific Avenue	Mary Bradford	149
Song Of The Triple OG Bird Rescue Man	Robert Lashley	150
We Are Tacoma	Steve Nebel	152
Ode	Nakanée Fernandez	154
This	Mae Murray-Angstadt	156
A View of Tacoma	Aisha Lawson	157
Eagles Every Day	Elizabeth Bradfield	158
CONTRIBUTORS		159
CREDITS		170

INTRODUCTION

To write a poem, or anything for that matter, about a particular place takes a lot of careful thought. It takes time and space. Time in the place and the space to think about it. It requires presence. It requires grace.

In the process of helping to develop the community of writers who created this anthology I had the chance to witness, through time and space, the magic that happens when these elements creatively converge. Congeal. Coagulate.

In that time and space I worked with a lot of amazing people. People who I had previously called friends and people I met who I can now also call friends. Poets, Artists, Thinkers, Dreamers, Editors, Publishers; all with an opinion and some with advice. This community is an amazing place.

It started with an idea that took root after a meeting with Michael Haeflinger in late 2022. We met at Campfire Coffee and the idea I had for an anthology grew and grew as we bounced ideas off of one another. This process replicated many times over in the several months as I did the same brainstorming with Chris Vega, Kristy Gledhill, Lisa Lewis, Cameron Combs, Adela Ramos, Jackie Casella, Jenny Bartoy, Naomi Strom-Avila, and many other creatives and literary thinkers in the Tacoma area.

After the project was chosen for the Tacoma Artists Initiative Program grant in 2023 we continued to have conversations about what this project meant, what we could do to not only create an anthology but help support the existing literary arts community. Conversations continued within the community as we stretched to achieve our goal of truly representing the Voices of Tacoma. To that end, a community conversation in February, 2024, with the folks at the Hilltop Urban Garden (HUG) was pivotal.

We had just closed for submissions and had 60+ poets who contributed, which was fantastic. But the racial demographics were overwhelmingly white, compared to the demographics of Tacoma. As I presented the demographics to the folks at HUG they were clear - this project anthology could not be published, or claim to represent Tacoma, without a more equitable representation of BIPOC poets.

We reopened to BIPOC poets immediately and, when we closed for submissions a second time, we had more equitable representation. It was truly the community conversation that pushed us to look back on our mission to represent the City, and I am grateful for the folks who spoke the truth. It wasn't perfect – we missed getting a representative group of Hispanic, Latino, or Spanish poets – so we know where we need to focus in the future.

Project Demographics	Results	Tacoma 2020 Census
African American / Black	11%	11%
Asian	10%	9%
Hispanic, Latino, or Spanish	6%	12%
Indigenous or Native American	7%	2%
Native Hawaiian or Pacific Islander	1%	1%
White	40%	57%
Two or or more races	17%	13%
Other	7%	4%

We also were very focused on getting a range of voices from across our city. Though submissions were open to poets anywhere in the world, the majority came from the greater-Tacoma area.

When we plotted the ZIP codes of contributors on a map we saw a large concentration in Central Tacoma and the Hilltop, which was fantastic. But what we were missing was a better distribution of contributors - we missed getting any poets from the Lincoln District and we only had two poets from the Eastside, which is, by population, the largest neighborhood in our city.

We learned a lot of lessons in the process of creating this anthology. We learned the value of community building (with monthly gatherings, events, workshops, and hundreds of hours of outreach in all corners of the city), and we learned amazing things about our City through the voices of the poets - as will the readers of this anthology.

The anthology would not have been possible without the work of the editorial review board which included Julie Baldock, Jenny Bartoy, Teshawn Deville, Kristy Gledhill, Michael Haeflinger, Joanne Rixon, Celeste Schueler, Katharine Threat, Josie Emmons Turner, and Jesi Vega. I am grateful for their time and dedication to reading and scoring each of the poems, along with editorial suggestions and input. I am also grateful for the work of Delvis George, who interned on the project and helped develop ideas for further outreach and social media campaigns.

Lastly I want to thank Mauricio Robalino for being such an amazing partner in this work. Mauricio's visual art is truly poetic and is very much in the spirit of our City, with images that strike the viewer with the strength, beauty, and grit that Tacoma is known for.

Burl E. Battersby
Tacoma, Washington, July 2024

Submissions by Neighborhood

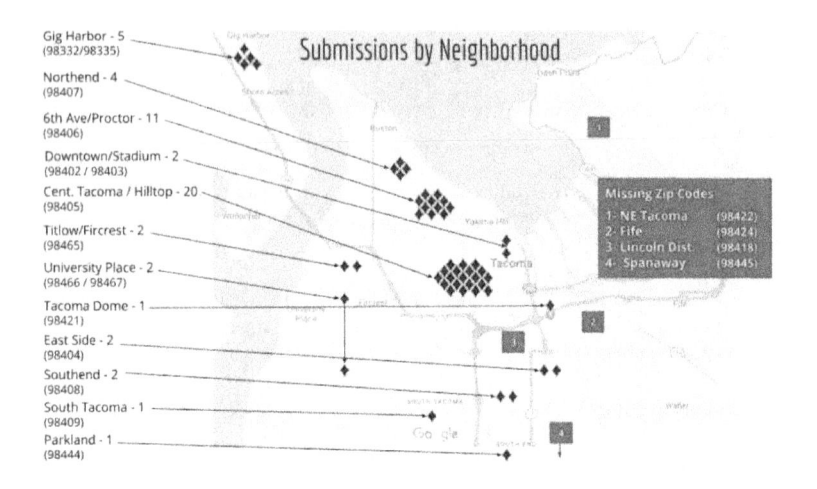

- Gig Harbor - 5 (98332/98335)
- Northend - 4 (98407)
- 6th Ave/Proctor - 11 (98406)
- Downtown/Stadium - 2 (98402 / 98403)
- Cent. Tacoma / Hilltop - 20 (98405)
- Titlow/Fircrest - 2 (98465)
- University Place - 2 (98466 / 98467)
- Tacoma Dome - 1 (98421)
- East Side - 2 (98404)
- Southend - 2 (98408)
- South Tacoma - 1 (98409)
- Parkland - 1 (98444)

Missing Zip Codes
1. NE Tacoma (98422)
2. Fife (98424)
3. Lincoln Dist. (98418)
4. Spanaway (98445)

Chapter 1

Redlined
Frank D'Andrea

After the orcas
Dart back to deep, fur remains
surf-stained Owen Beach.

Tahoma Doesn't Love Us
Abby E. Murray

The Puyallup River salmon
are not addressed to us
and neither are the owls.
The mountain isn't wearing
white for us, won't blush
because we came to see it.
Daffodils and maples pull
gold from the ground here
without our pleasure in mind
and when we slice pine trees
into planks, Tahoma says
no prayer for us, a people.
The tideflats shrug reflections
of our shipyard toward
the shore in favor of the sky
and all its moods—cornflower
and smoke season and a veil
of sodium vapor orange—
fabric it holds like a mother
day and night, mending it
with black fins that rise
and sink around each tear
like threaded needles. Tahoma
wears each season like a pin
it knows it will lose and does.
It is older than churches
and railroads and destiny,
too ancient for our naming,
its pulse deep in some wrist
we cannot grab and twist.
Isn't that some comfort? Its heart
is wild around us, too present
to pledge itself to our roots.
And you and I are animals
as good at digging and taking
as we are at loving instead.

[original poem, published in *Grit City Magazine*, December 2020]

April
render jemis

i want to carry life upon my head
like a basket of groceries in spring
on the walk from the Safeway on M,

                              like the snow of cherry blossoms
                              coming to rest on my locs after frolic,
                              i want to carry life upon my head.

i want to carry life upon my head
and the faint gingery smell of my
neighbors' magnolias in my nose.

                              like the wind lifts the fiery chant
                              for freedom from every campus heart,
                              i want to hoist life upon my very head.

i want to carry life upon my head
like your scent on borrowed shirt,
like your seashell on green altar cloth,

                              like the cloud cap halo rests
                              on mount Tacoma, mother of waters,
                              i want to carry life upon my head.

At the Source of the Ore Our Smelter Processed, Thus Making Commencement Bay a Superfund Site (or) At Least the Tailings of a Glacier Are, if not Beautiful, not Toxic
Elizabeth Bradfield

        On the glacier above Kennecott Mine, melt pool
        a pure Listerine at my feet. Clouds & shadows. Distance
        unhighwayed, unbridged. No matter the nationality,
        everyone on the trail speaks gear: crampon, ripstop.
        The red mine buildings are charming, an attraction
        giving scale, held by policy in "arrested decay."
        Toward the ablating glacier's foot, the ice is tired, grey.

It was not pretty in Tacoma.
Sure, there were nice spots, parks
and a few of the beaches. Some historic `
structures like the jail were quaint.
But, really, we were pulp
mill, dockyards, smelter.

        The gift shop, a replica of the store
        where miners paid their bosses
        for what they needed, displays empty crates
        of Washington apples. Warm, tart sun
        sent north when ships came up for copper ore.

We fished, swam, ate clams that sucked
the water of the bay into their soft bodies.
No harm to report. The smelter's gone,
the stack that was our horizon mark
for the sun's swing, imploded.
Guys in hazmat suits cleaned the site
for years. Horsetails frond the tailings.

        Above treeline, the contact zone is clear:
        A line where two rocks meet—limestone,
        greenstone—and minerals precipitate. The miners
        slept there, bunkrooms frosted by breath,
        shaft left cold so they'd work harder. Porphyry's
        jagged ridge is stunning, but they wouldn't have seen it
        from so close. I bet most of them

hated it here, where it still
is beautiful. I bet they
couldn't wait to get out either.

At St. Leo's
Katherine Van Eddy

I have been many people there:
college student, newlywed, mother
of one, then two, then separated,
divorced, pregnant and engaged again.
Twenty years of a life.

On the Hilltop, we meet
in the basement of what was once
a massive church with four spires,
built to be noticed, but burned.
The basement was meant

to be temporary, but remained,
restored, with stained glass
windows and grey rivers etched
in the plain flooring. I like the
unevenness of it,

how we can show up as we are,
listen to the water trickling
in the baptismal font, wash
one another's feet, become
another flame in the story.

Sonnenizio on Orchard Street
After John Ashbury
Micah Ackerman Hirsch

it's bankruptcy, the human haul, on the day someone sells an old house -
like as if to know the recursive of what makes a life (which is the same old story as ever),
same as whenever the old computers were torn down and packed away
and the knitted memory unwound. it gets old, of course it does -
living loves you never quite kick, the binary bits, the city zoo gone old and overgrown,
the names and lives of arsenic and fog and fir. but i guess my old man,
you know, he loved sunday mornings at the market in a town that's now my old town,
in a life that's now my old life. and the recombinant years, how they build the infrastructure
and all the random accessories of grief: bless the old remembering of how it came to be.
blessing to sit on porches damp with age and drink the same old plum brandy and tea,
and remember the days before you could hear the magnetic dead, like old-ringed trees,
wait in silence to be known. and that was love then i suppose, like when lovers grow old,
like when old lovers go. and what is it to listen to the dead on wires and tapes and code?
signaling the days of old, when living was a slow unwinding of everything you'd ever known.

Red Elm Cafe on MLK Jr. Way
Andrea Clausen

The sweet bitter scent of coffee and waffles,
gone. The soft chatter and the older man
sitting on the couch knitting, gone.

But the red elm tree on plate glass was steadfast.
No going out of business sign.
No boarded up windows, or bare floors,
lone light bulb hanging from high ceiling.

In the year of shut down, shut up,
shut in, the year when breath
became death, masks mandatory,
and hugging taboo, I fingered my fully
punched coffee card. Found it as a happy
mistake and considered mocha,
caramel, and cinnamon because,
in that year of without, whenever I could
finally stash my mask and smile with
more than my eyes, I knew my old order,
black coffee no room for cream,
would not be enough.

Now, I think about my 46th year
coming up in a few days, how
the sister-owners might stick a candle
in my whipped cream covered waffle,
ask how the bike ride over was while
shaking rainbow sprinkles on top,
and sing me into a new year.

Walking with the Birder at Wapato Park
For Kelsey
Celeste Maria Schueler

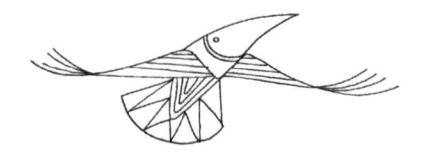

Silence of the birder—— Wapato Park,
Eagles in the evergreen,
this poem cannot hold your hand slick from rain——
look into sky through binoculars,
observe the sun curious as a cat between clouds.
Fingers caught in pine——roaring cedars——
silence of the birder gazing across water——
gazing across black eye of crow, cawing on powerline,
calling into rain.
Ripples across Wapato as we walk in silence,
listening only to birds beyond evergreen.

November 3, 1885
Melody Derrick

"This business is nothing but talk."
Three pairs embroidered shoes.
Ten chickens.
A pair of boots.
One silk umbrella.
Woolen blankets.
A business and good will thereof amounting in value of $2,000.
"The wind was blowing a gale. It was raining hard."
A one-story framed building.
Rice, beans, pigs, a vegetable garden.
Six silk handkerchiefs.
Black cotton trousers.
One feather mattress.
Medicines.
"I took about $2 worth of bread to feed some of the Chinese who were my relatives."
Silk trousers, women's.
Brick yard, buildings.
Ten blue cotton shirts.
Two red woolen bed covers.
Two tables, six chairs, one large mirror.
"The mob put many of my things in wagons and carried them away."
Mrs. May's mind,
her sanity.
One clock.

It Feels Like
Liz Morrow

The burning kick of
whisky sliding down the back of
your throat,
the smell of wildfire
and gasoline exhaust,
frigid waves lapping
at your feet,
buckled concrete bowing
to the power of cedar
roots,
steam and fog settling
amidst gantry cranes
illuminated like
cotton candy in the
morning light,
the bitter pleasure of
black coffee and
cigarette smoke.

You Have an Accent
Jessica J. Bloodsaw

Words are different here;
maybe it's the rain.
It moistens the tongues,
chokes the voice
of the utterers, that silence

doubters, allows storytellers
to whisper their sweet nectar
into the honeycomb ears
of those who claim
the rights of the land

they stole, from the Native
givers honored by
the acknowledgment
but never the return,
always the intent

to make it great again,
though it never was
(who chooses) what's
truth, what's shared,
what's remembered

(who chooses) the narrative
in the tape deck
of our shared humanity
in the ever-green environs,
be kind; rewind

to the beginning
of the ages, where there
is only light and dark,
the sun and the moon,
the stars and the ocean

before Rainier,
before Mount Tahoma,
Cascadia, the sound—Puget,
the sound—zap-zinger
wind shocks the bridge

that binds blended worlds,
destitute with destiny,
all in the city, the annex,
the unincorporated
(whose) nouns share hate

and ignorance, enlightenment
and love, (whose) verbs
express long days and short
years in the song-notes
of the sound—Puget,

sound—zap-zinger
wind shocks the language,
words are different
here; maybe
it's the rain

Today there is a breeze and nothing is on fire...
Michael Haeflinger

Today there is a breeze and nothing is on fire.
The party decorations still hang on the house.
Balloons strung from makeshift lattice across the yard.
A banner over the door reflecting the afternoon sun.
Traffic is light today. No one shouting or fighting.
No hot rods percussing Yakima. No sirens.
Whatever songs the birds sing in the leaves, robust.
They dot the breeze's dialogue, the dogs barking.
Neighbors come out and go back in. Some speak.
Most don't. The air is flavorless and swift.
It moves hammocks. It brings the early evening to everyone.
It encourages Camellia flowers to dance for no one.
Balloons steady themselves against the side of the house
While far off forests, still wet with winter
Stay just where they belong.

Elders Rage At Snake Lake After A Shootout
Robert Lashley

Reflection, on the Lake
is a ripple that eats
then spits out an outline of the woods.
The women in black dip their old tambourines
then blur away from it.
The old men tie their suits into knots
then blur away from it
The people join and move their hands
To deny his name in the cold.
    "the water spirit brought us.
   "The water spirit will not bring us home"
They wash the memory of blood in ice
And cry power in the darkness
  "the water spirit will not bring us home
Hums turn to shouts and chants re woven
and moans play in scale with the squirrel bounce.
  "the water spirit will not bring us home"
Frogs jump a beat back from their hand claps.
Night bugs swarm but cannot trace steps
in an array of burying grounds
of shadows and spirits in the water.
The juba clap is the overriding veil
of sirens and funeral pyres.
The gunshot at night is the eleventh plague
so they part this iteration of the sea.
    "the water spirit brought us.
   "The water spirit will not bring us home"

spearmint
Gloria Joy Kazuko Muhammad

maple, ash, cypress
become spearmint *overnight*

    glasses clink and fireworks blast
    snowflakes dazzle wide and vast

        our houseless family

        on ***windows*** and ***roofs***

        our family in dis-ease

        on ***windows*** and ***roofs***

ferry, mckinley, wright
become spearmint overnight

        augmented reality paints the needle's sky
        our needle can't stitch the most basic of threads

gift wrapping in landfills

landfills making earth

    s
     a
      d

        this isn't seasonal affective

    this is
          w
         a
          r

spearmint gives us its sweetness
    and

    then

        d i s a p *p* *e* *a* *r* *s*

red hood, white hood, blue hood
Albert de Santis

There's a dull red pickup's been
in the neighbor's sideyard all year
The hood's clear coat crisped
like peeling sunburn spackled
by a local convocation
Eagles of a pilgarlic persuasion
or more like birds with beer guts
who crap like cooked white eggs
on red dinner plates
That truck hasn't moved all winter
and here it is now spring
and evermore the eyesore
it's hood more white than red

Today we get a break
your mother showed up late
better than never
to save our sanity
watch our colicky baby
so we get a moment to ourselves
only he falls asleep immediately
engulfed by her breasty dress.
Figures. and now that we're
outside, it's pouring down rain.

That shitty pickup's been took to town
I said to you. I watched the tow truck
work at dawn while the little one
was bawlin' on my arm cuz
when he didn't sleep
neither'd no one.

Now in the early afternoon
there's a different car
parked there
new and unfamiliar
Each rain drop stands defiant
on the waxed blue hood
we'll see how long that lasts

We shiver in the cold and rain
sharin a smoke under the wet
white red and blue standard
protruding from the porch post
smoke clouds unfurl from my white hood
into your big ass hair curlers
hopeful we'll catch a matinee
We chat but it feels like it's killing
time talking about the weather,
and what's changed in the hood.

its just that
all morning the sun had shown
and I just sat rusting inside
and now that i'm out the door
I'm still not moving
like i'm just waiting
for the truck to tow
for the sun to show
but the rain is
and my heart isn't
but i am
but i know
it's going to change
i just don't know how

Chapter 2

Charro 4 Charro
Vaquero Azul

The crackle of leather against another
The click of my botas as I dance upon the floor
Your delicious laughter as we twirl underneath the velvet stars
We joke about being "Charro 4 Charro" our "T4T"
A woman wearing a Folklorico skirt with Trans flag ribbons
Kisses a woman with Bi colored flores de papel in her hair
The fire illuminates our faces as we share tales
"I never had this as a kid/ I dreamed of things like this/
Ojalá tuviera esto mientras crecía"
Spanglish is spoken with giggles and not a single ounce of shame
Our corazones have all the love we never received
Pouring out in luscious red, hands open
"Ven aquí mi amor, bailemos toda la noche."

Today's Tacoma
Andrea Clausen

Cranes dot the skyline, fly
high into cumulus clouds
sounds bouncing off brick,
thick and crowding out fast
last light of the day. Oh,
so you thought I meant wings,
things feathered and beaked, not
hot black smoke choking out
shouts from the school next door.
Four, well more now, high-rises
size up the small family homes,
nowhere to plant the backyard
far-walled garden anymore. Yes,
guesses are right, prices are rising,
buyers from Seattle seizing up land
hand over hand and we, solid middle class
cast doubt on how we will ever afford
more than an apartment. Sure, urban density
fences in folks, cuts down commutes, but
what about us who just want the three bedrooms,
room for two, but on our own land. No dogs
hogging our shared yard, barking above us,
chewing through old balls. Cute as they are, we
see them and wonder if we will ever have walls,
hallways, a room where rent won't rise and,
standing on the front porch, we can say "Our home."

Stopped and Frisked at University Place Suicide Blues
Robert Lashley

(with a nod to Yeats)

"Or does it explode?"
        —Langston Hughes, *"What Happens to a Dream Deferred"*

Or does it escape you?
Does it leave—quietly—
in the sudden declines of September—
by synonyms of nature
and circles of cars
and men who plead your body like the drums—
men who plead your blood long after your skin
        lies in its veneer of matter.

Here, the cops dream your Ladean body,
with grit wings beating and staggering gate—
with webs, fingers and terrifying napes
as your figure gets limp by the tree—
as the vagueness of hands among members
become hurdles to plausible beatings—
as your body laid in their white rushes
feel the strange hands where frisking lies—
as the safety illusion of your loins
is sacrificed on unbroken walls
and open car roofs, caught up in the games
and brut blood of the friskers stroll
and your lobotomized silence survival.

And after they finish, will the sun have too much light?
Will the breeze and all its subtexts
violate your space?
Will the willow trouble your mind ?
Will the evergreens—fixed
In their portable promised lands—
color a life you'll never have again?

Where am I
B. Eugene B.

I am called by names
    Which don't describe me,
    But intend, instead,
To bind me.
    While
Buffeted & burnished by inertia,
    One-hundred-fifty-eight-thousand
    Encircle me
    At seventy miles an hour.
Their motion perpetual,
    Running on impervious pavement,
    Cutting past what was once
    A prairie, a swamp, & a cemetery.
I am defined
    By these spiraling routes,
    By a midtown vortex.
But I am not defined
    Only by that
    Which has grown inside me.
Rather than be characterized by my crossroads
    They are incisions which create
    My four sections.
Within me are two overlooks,
    One prospects a Friend's meeting place,
    One crests on a road called Montana
        Embracing the Islamic Center.
Come seek a loop inside me
    Connecting my parts back together again.
We are here placemaking
    Emerging from past to present,
    Hoping to be peace bearing
    We find our future
    For the taking.
So let us make the pavement porous.
    Let us connect sidewalks together.
Let us make it so we can again
    Count the cars that drive by.

Witness
Josie Emmons Turner

Seals arrive at high tide, tell us Coho,
Chum, are returning, threading their

way through that too small Crescent Creek
culvert, thoughtlessly built decades ago.

They are not deterred; they leave
eggs. Seals swim, watch. Eagles

spy. In November dark, this afternoon's
reddening, yellowing light, we watched

an eagle's split-second catch, a Chum.
That flapping fish seemed to fly, yearning,

fighting to swim again, when seal jumped,
caught its tale, pulled it into its own mouth.

Eagle screamed. Our tea kettle whistles.
Our afternoon, once again, settled

Tacoma…
Beverly Mathews

Where the sky is blue,
Unless it's raining, then it's gray.
But that's OK, I like it that way.

The Otters of Chambers-Clover Creek
Claudia Riiff Finseth

River otters slide loopy-backed
Across my frozen little pond
On Spanaway-Chambers-Clover Creek.

Break dancers on a floor of melting ice,
Rubbing, rolling, hugging the pond,
Long, heavy tails like ship rudders.

Scratching ears with webbéd feet,
Nose-kissing with twitching whiskers,
Quick cuddle, mom and pups.

Then on the run again, they
Slither off the edge and disappear
Under ice in a game of tag.

A water pocket twenty yards on boils,
Paw-scrubbed faces emerge
And now they float like clouds,

Sniff the air, and slip out again,
For more games on the ice,
And me watching still as stone.

Dear Ancestor
Christina Vega

I've been thinking diaspora / genocide / uncut roses
I've been real marimacha & scared
fire walking under full moon
wolves everywhere & rotting flowers
the only way we know to live
under threat

I want to pull them from the den
this powerlessness
a lesson no one needs

I've been taking deep breaths
imagining clear cielo on the mesa
air so clean it washes over me in a metal basin
scrubs me limb by limb on the front porch
I used to sleep without fear

I've been thinking about Reyna
her open palms razed
how she used to cook at the stove but doesn't eat
she's too resilient

a worked copper bowl
tamped metal & divots / empty pelvis / wiped clean
she's like that

Reyna is an interesting bowl
open mouth
abundant desert sky

After Tacoma | After Lewes
Micah Ackerman Hirsch

God don't sell me anything. I just want to live in a pale yellow house.
God don't sell me anything. I just want to live in a pale yellow house,
and write heartbreaking things. Breathe. Turn autumn's apples into jam
and write heartbreaking things. Breathe. Turn autumn's apples into jam.
Don't write heartbreaking things. Sell me anything: a pale yellow house,
autumn's apples, jam, God. I just want to live, breathe in and turn

    my raven, lone deer between the freeways in the morning.
    My raven, lone deer between the freeways in the morning.
    Four miles of automobiles along the curving Sound.
    Four miles of automobiles along the curving Sound.
    The Sound, my raven curving between the freeways in the morning:
    Deer along the automobiles. Four lone miles.

Now something simple - that's all. Kissing against trees. Collapsing down 30th Street.
Now something simple, that's all. Kissing against trees. Collapsing down 30th Street.
Anything that you could imagine.
Anything that you could imagine.
Imagine something that simple now. Anything. That's all.
Collapsing down against trees? Kissing 30th street? You could.

I just want to live in a pale yellow house.
God, now 30th street collapsing -
in the morning the curving Sound, autumn's apples down
four miles of freeways, lone automobiles tracing heartbreaking things
against trees. And breathe. Write. Turn into something simple. Anything that you could imagine,
my raven, that's all. Jam. Kissing. The deer between. (Don't sell me anything.)

Rain
Abbie Hughes

```
                    p
                    it
                   ter
                  pitter
               patter  tiptoes
              on window pane
             toadstools yawn a morn
            ing greeting   haplessly clinging
           to sodden trees     a mingling of
         pine needles gather in the sidewalk's hills
          and valleys   oh how they twist and corkscrew
          watch us move above the fog      a firm horizon
         denied by mist        grandfather cedars heave huge sighs
         into the heavens         a raven's shadow calls us home
         the flock pulls together              like a winced eye
         dear sunlight we missed your clean throw rugs beating on the bay
         as I squat with a mug of smoky tea      listening to the one
             sparrow claim his undisputed terrain      over and over
             I observe the puddle stompers        and avoiders
                but always muddled socks      climb mushy feet
                one must salute the wide canopy as it shields
                  many beings from the summer rain cover
                      ing the wetlands like a mother's
                            ever so calming
                                 hand
```

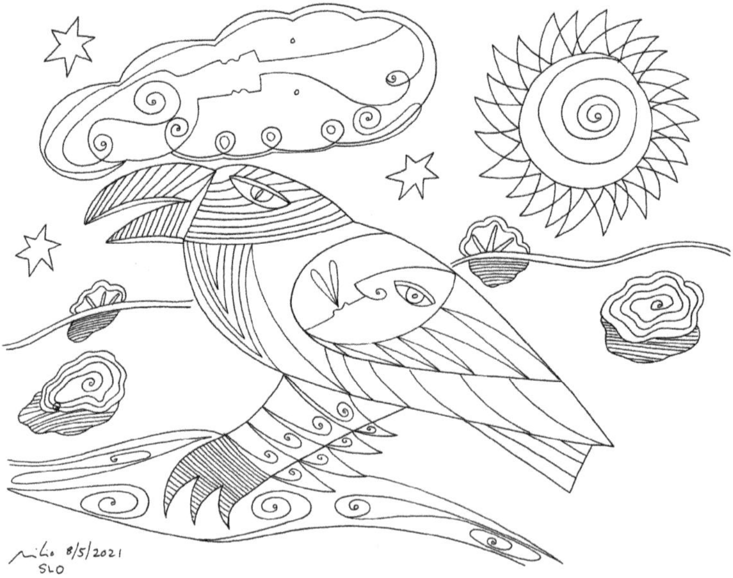
8/5/2021
SLO

Call It Futures
For Matt
Micah Ackerman Hirsch

For imagining you, hair slicked back, day dream
Of the Titlow silences, of the autocurrent emptiness,
In the 2x4 comfort of a pink stuccoed duplex,
A front porch full of highlighters,
A little apartment in the garden -
Something like that Jester's Crown on my desk,
Something like that fir along the fence.

    Your face at the window in the morning,
        Downwind from the sunlight.
    Reposed in the shadow of the 16 West,
        Whatever we leave to stand.

        Your voice calling down the beveled coastlines.
        Your voice calling out across the sightlines.

            Your face in the garden painting figures,
            Teaching all the imitating hands.
            Reposed in the shadow of the 16 West,
                Whatever we leave to stand.

                For imagining you, hair slicked back, day dream
                Of what we call a future over telephone wires
                And satellite poles. Sweet talking down the renegades
                ,Between all the losts and founds
                .Between all the steps to take
                ,Something like that pothos on the balcony
                .Something like that lavender, way out in that high-noon shade

WHAT'S IN A NAME?
Anida Yoeu Ali

My name is
2,000 years of history present in 1 body
        3 decades of civil unrest awake in 3 syllables
                5 letters dense of Birth   Blood   Islam   Peace   Khmer   Story
        2 letters away from 'Refugee'
1 letter short of 'Home'

My name knows my mother labored
        screaming for hours
               only to mourn a year later
as she buried her sorrow.
A baby boy
  empty of breastmilk
        born into famine *instead* of family.
                (2 letters and war separate the difference)
  My mother buried the pains from her first labor
        along with her grief,   knowing
                her son had learned the word for hunger
                      before he was able to call her 'mother' or speak her name.
        She labored a second time and my name was born.
My name unexpectedly inherited first child honors.
My name echoes the same *shahadah** whispered to newborns

When you say my name
        it is a prayer   a mantra   a call

when you say my name
I respond.

Before countries bounded themselves into borders
        before cities became governments
               even before the nations of hip hop
it is the original call and response that all people claim.

So I take issue with *your* inarticulate mangling of my name
she refuses to disintegrate into a colonized tongue.

My name survived racism before she knew what it was called.
A small child sinks deeper into her seat
      into her shame
              into her difference
                    into *their* laughter
               into *their* stares
       into *their* sneers
into a classroom of white kids
            with white teachers

                        with white tongues
                                with perfectly pronounceable white American names
                                        like Katy, Courtney, Jennifer,
                                Michael, Bobby, Doug,
                        Mrs. Smith, Mrs. Nelson
                    Mr. How-do-you-say-your-weird-name again?
Miss I'm-sorry-I-just-can't-seem-to-say-it-right!

Every mispronunciation is like a mouth shooting bullets
                triggers *precise* memories attached to *precise* feelings
like shame inflected in my parents' broken English
        and the guilt of witnessing
                their dreams and youth slaughtered for money, food, *my* perfect English.
Every misplaced tongue targets *my* foreignness, *my* un-belonging, *my* vulnerabilities.
So when I get angry or curse you for your mispronunciation
        Please don't tell me I can't do that
                Don't tell me to take it easy
                        Don't scold me afterwards for making a point of it in public
Don't shrink me down any further
Please just listen.

Allow me to own this one thing:
The rights to my name.
        to say her correctly
                to have her said correctly
                        to come when she calls me
                                to come to her defense
                                        to live up to her
                                                to honor her legacy.
She is my only refuge when I am stripped naked.
        She is my bloodline to mothers who have labored before me.
                She is My Name. The echo of Home I long to remember.
My name is *Anida*
   daughter of *Surayya*
      who is the daughter of *Abidah*
        who is the daughter of *Fatimah*
          who is the daughter of a woman whose name I do not know
            who are all daughters of *Hawwa*
                daughters of life
                    sisters of survival
                        women of resistance
                            descendants of earth
                                    water
                                        breath
                                            fire
                                                dreams.

*shahadah – A Muslim's declaration of faith

Surroundings
Roxann Murray

White houses with black trim
These new structures obstruct my view
Old homes demolished in the name of development
On my walks, more and more are built.

I flee to the Point
To be surrounded by green
The trees and moss comfort me
When I don't want to see anything manmade.

Down on the waterfront
Cormorants rest on the ship's steel wires
At sunset, they gently sway in the breeze
While drivers pass by without noticing.

Squeeze
Katherine Van Eddy

One day a year, Curran Apple Orchard is open to all.
We wait in a snaking line over an hour to reach the press,
and it's worth it to see my son's face as he turns the crank,

sending pieces of wet apple flesh flying into the air,
squeezing a couple gallons of tart cider from our crate
of palm-sized apples newly plucked from low branches

because we are amateurs here, without the proper tools,
like a ladder, a fruit picker basket, or the power to freeze
time and my children just this way, for longer than a single,

fleeting season.

Rain Cycle Centered
Maizy Apple Green

Sublimation is when something goes straight from a solid state to a gaseous one,

skipping the liquid state all together

Sublimation happens to dry ice and at the top of Mount Everest so, while there is no doubting its

occurrence- it seems uncommon - especially in a state that is so rain cycle centered

Growing up in Washington State,

I learned the water cycle multiple times and the one I recall clearest involved

a diagram with a bay on the left, a hill on the right and clouds across the whole top of the page

In my head it was translucent water, silver from the sky washed shiny yet again

by moss on a forest floor trickling around roots of evergreen trees

and rocked softly by the undercurrents of all the different inlets and bays I grew up around

In reality it is the rain from rooftops to gutters to California Trimmer cut lawns

That quartz glimmer of water is the most visible when it runs across pavement at night under a streetlamp

I learned about a system and once outside the classroom it looked different then I imagined it would

Field Notes:

Sublimation is phenomenon and precipitation is common here

Gold dust in the storm drains is unlikely but golden leaves in the storm drains are very likely

Fog that hangs on Commencement Bay is similar to the steam that rises off the car windshields

- but not the same

Sublimation happens to dry ice and at the top of Mount Everest

- so, I may not come across it for some time

And the water cycle is different than my elementary school imagination thought it would be

I learned about a system and once outside the classroom it looked different then I imagined it would

And yet there is still quartz, silver, and gold dust; fog and steam all the same

Between the bays and cut lawns, the rain still trickles between the roots of evergreen trees

It is still rain cycle centered

The water cycle lessons are still applicable to my own life

The fog on the bay is always mine, the overcast too

And I recite to myself "look just how green everything is when it rains"

Chapter 3

One Hundred Days of Solitude
Lucas Smiraldo

Aloneness arrives at
the speed of
the planets
crossing the coasts
and swallowing us
into shadows that shift
by the every minute
and I am not
the same life
I learned
by touch
and steering wheel
and casual breath
because nothing is
immune to
the random dew
of a passage
and the holding

this relentless
and necessary
holding
that swallows months
in it's limbs
but cannot embrace
a friend or
welcomed
stranger.

They say that one
of these
barged onto the
earth
a century
past and
I wonder if this
terrible pause
is the way
she wounds us
back so
that she can heal,
seizing time
and the air
around it

and distancing herself
from human
matters

while the sparrows
and the finches
and the starlings
take the morning
from us
along the delicate greed
of the
understory.

Here are my reports:

in 30 days fish
are returning to
the toxic
canals of Venice

the haze is lifting
from LA

I can cross 19th
street
on foot
without much wait.

Here are my reports:

One third of this city
cannot pay its rent

spouses and their children cringe
at the violations
stricken skin
and broken vessels
with little intermission
now
and so few
windows

a wife is forbidden
from the fingertips
of her lover/husband
of 30 years

as he gasps his final prayers

away from her

so far away.

These
are the arbitrary
laws that pock
the silence
and mark us
and force love
from our throats
like toothpaste
from a
minted tube
until our need for each other
spills all over
these awkward
and barely standing vessels
that were so pristine
just a month
ago.

Who knows
how long
these hundred
days will last?

The sidewalks have
bigger right of ways
people step aside
onto the grass strips
and wait for us
to
go
just go

the women in blue tear jeans
at the walk up coffee stand
is the priest
and the laughing sage
and greatest hope
for us all
as she
sets the cup
in the nurse's hand.

I am with you
in this –
alone-
apostles
of the web cam Zoom
listener
at the shrinking
tiny desk
with a purple moon
smiling across
the clearing
sky
and the thought
that nature
steals from us
what we
will not give
it

and we are
destined
to live
as both
its casualties

and saints.

The Worm Moon
Tanner Abernathy

If a unit of virus became the moon
we would keep smoking on midnight
porches and wishing for flannel
sheets.

The worm moon is a turmeric nipple
pressed against the pane of night.
My wife drives me to the top of 30th street.

Water carries the light, pauses,
and carries it again over Commencement Bay—
if the reflection was unbroken
something might come slouching down
to this gray brine city to be born
and nursed in the milk-fogged hills.

Soil in the valleys thaws and
writhes, pink in the moonglow.

At the Goldfish Tavern
Kevin Miller

No long walk on the short pier, this
short walk to the tavern in first sun.
Each day, the dog and I check the specials

board through the north window, ritual
like candles and wishes, toast and tea,
we look knowing today's special is

chicken sandwich and three years running.
The Rainier tall-can stays on the bar,
blackberry vines cross the window, wind

a domed Tom Robbins tribute, this bar
on stop-time, still life with park crows,
the ghosts of bikers, and each morning

the dog and I finish the menu's erased line.
Today *jello salad with marshmallows* completes
the elliptical chicken sandwich special.

Mother haunts Point Defiance.
Winter mornings we imagine seasonal sides
for the special— *oatmeal, eggs & hashbrowns,*

biscuits & gravy. Full disclosure, the biscuits
will be shaped like bones. We persist, this
daily pilgrimage, two morning drinkers.

On Mount Rainier
Meredith Smith

Barely a ghost on sun days,
She breaks through clouds,
She argues for space and sky,

She looks down upon

    the ageless seas,
    the speeding boats,
    the busy people,
    and the aching world below.

She doesn't know what it's good for.

Year's End Wright Park
Kevin Miller

I am a black coat to the shadows
at the windows turning
from east wing hospital beds.
The puddles on this path are ice,
and last night's dusting of powder
swirls cross-surface like mercury
I scattered on my school desk.
Sister Clarice's talk of mortal sin
drove me to the thermometer's heart.
Each quicksilver touch multiplied
every time I tried to stop the poison.
The pencil tray's thin ditch offered
one last chance for reconciliation.
Winter opens in, I see the wind's way,
last leaves hang like lost mittens,
ice fog makes rime on the rind of snow
glazing branches. Nests float like inkblots—
every empty bowl a success.

All that is solid and melts must end up somewhere
William Kupinse

I'd stolen the afternoon's late winter hour
to cycle through the neighborhood and the next.
Each pedal-turn turned over in my mind
what flashed past right and left:
old houses with the same new paint
—white clapboards, black trim—
like character actors all made up as mimes.

My reflections on private equity's public harm
came to a halt as I swerved hard
before a glassy shimmer in the road.
Too warm out for black ice, I steered around it just in case,
but the glimmer shone there too, in the places
where the road had moments earlier seemed dry.
Against that scintillation, my tires could find no traction
and soon bicycle and I were sliding sideways down the street.

The asphalt finally grabbed us at the far shore of the shimmer,
where I touched a finger to the strange translucent stuff.
It was slippery but also somehow viscous
and a thousand filaments glowed like molten sugar
when I pulled apart my finger from my thumb.
Good grief, I thought, that's just my luck
to hit a patch of late stage capitalism.

The phone I'd been unsuccessful at losing
rang in my back pocket. My friend John was calling,
so I answered from beneath the bike, still sprawled across the street.

Hey Bill, you won't believe this, but I was walking down to City Hall
to make a public comment, only to be stopped
by a flood of some crazy stuff rising like a tide up Market Street.
It's liquid yet it's hard, it's there and then it's not,
and if I scoop some in a glass, the glass dissolves
and the substance takes its shape. Weird, huh?

John, I said, *you've got to get out of there.*
That rising tide's a municipal leak of late stage capitalism.

No sooner had my friend exclaimed *Bejeebus*!
the university text alert arrived:

WE ARE AWARE THAT THE POOLING SUBSTANCE IN THE QUAD
CONTINUES TO RISE. FACILITIES IS DOING
ITS BEST TO CONTAIN THE SITUATION.
OUR TEAM OF BRAND CONSULTANTS HAS DETERMINED
THAT THE SUBSTANCE PRESENTS NO IMMEDIATE DANGER,
BUT THEY AGREE THAT IT IS SLIPPERY AND STICKY
AND THAT ITS AROMA OF CINNABON AND CYANOACRYLATE GLUE IS CONFUSING
AND ALSO THAT IT DISSOLVES SYNTHETIC FABRICS.

I scrolled to the end of the wall of text:

OUT OF AN ABUNDANCE OF CAUTION,
ADMINISTRATORS IN FIRST-FLOOR OFFICES
WILL BE RELOCATED TO HIGHER GROUND.

I tried to call my wife, but the screen
melted beneath my fingers. So too
my bicycle tire was sighing out its air.

As I pushed the bike back home,
I could hear up in the higher branches
the crows and jays speculating
just what would happen next.

Eat My Food
Felicia Tran

We chew and swallow this again and again.
We move forward but we won't move on.
We turn the discard into delicacies.

They thought it was poison and garbage.
They thought we were poison and garbage.
We show them we know how to eat what seems inedible
because we know how to prepare delicious things from remnants,
from imperfection.

We are not deluded
And will not be diluted.
We know how the world works.

Now they eat my food with delight
And discuss the ghosts of their disgust.

Migration Song
Kristy Gledhill

Wet Wisconsin windshield wipering by,
cheese curds and the Polka Jubilee bounced
her into the west. Bounced and weeping
westward to a new home, across the green-
banked Mississippi—sprawled and bleeding into
her journal—westward ho! She wasn't ready.

Never been ready. Still not ready, but ready's
overrated. Long live that girl, who wanted Dusty
Rose lips and cowboy boots for the trip, but who
settled for netting dead guppies into the Sioux Falls
Kmart parking lot from the backseat aquarium,
stumping in to fetch fish flakes on her broken
right ankle, its flat boot, its reminder and burden.

Long live her not knowing, that girl, her blank-page
not-knowingness, her right-now and her guppy net,
her cut-up boot-cuts, broken leg over the console.
Long live the South Dakota squint, the ghost stag
leading Billings to Bozeman, Yakima's bait and switch
breakdown (*This is Washington?!*) and finally the black-
green Cascades descent, rain-chased, two days past
turnaround time, first salt smell and deep jagged sky.

Long live that girl's heart on day one, peeking over
the sill into tall firs and their jet blue jays whose
not-quite-rightness, their raucous newness and oily
sheen brought tears for the jays she'd known. Tacoma.
The twisted madrona. All of it. Long live it. Long live
its unknownness and flame, its open hand in hers.

Haiku of Destiny
Tia Pliskow

Mr. Carr's garden
Planted and cultivated
At the railway's end

On the #1 Bus
Mary Bradford

Whatever happened to unobstructed views?
Who decided it was a good idea to slap advertisements on bus windows?
Will it ever stop raining?
As the #1 bus trundled down 6th Avenue
on a soakingly grim Sunday,
passengers were few,
the air was thick with moist, shared breath,
and I had questions . . .
questions that were abruptly interrupted
when the bus lurched to a stop
at 6th and Stevens.
The doors swung open, and our driver announced
that there was a vivid double-rainbow
hanging just behind us.
We should all hop off to take a look, he said.
And so it was that an improbable Holy Trinity gathered that day:
a silver-crowned crone, a testy teen with a nose ring of gold,
and our mild-mannered driver ~
transformed for an instant into our High Priest of Awe ~
all standing next to the #1 bus on 6th Avenue,
savoring the unexpected,
the fleeting hues of mystery,
the arcing brilliance of colors split . . .
before they dissolved back into the drear
and the bus ride continued
on a Sunday that was no longer grim.

She Comes to School
Josie Emmons Turner

She comes to school

sometimes.

Her thick brown hair, in a bun.
Her Lavalava* over jeans.
Her flip-flops rain soaked.

She stops coming.
Her phone is out of order.
Letters home unanswered.

We look up her address.
Pass burned-out trailer courts.
Artillery booms from the Base.

We circle her street.
She comes to the door, rubs her eyes.
She's surprised to see teachers.

She comes to school the next day.
She stops again.
Her mother was not released.

Someone must care for the baby.

*a Lavalava is a Samoan cotton wrap, tied at the waist.

Hold No Bitterness
Sandra K. King

The skittish heels of my mind wish to toddle backward on worries' spiral path,
away from transition's tottering ledge.
I inventory a pocket full of strung marble beads;
tally up the rings of a felled tree and understand.
Time is short.

Flying stones of retaliation--
the cost of getting on with it—
are nothing over which to get fed up.
It's the minutes wasted being vexed over them
that will eat you alive.
I shake the pebbles of futility out of fragility's mournful shoes.

It's been weeks since I saw the tree--
its branches clothed in bark itching with new buds
having spent glorious days with its velvety mossy green
sun-drenched arms reaching up to the dusky, periwinkle sky.

The thought of this sends a dawdling scarlet wave
brain-ward,
as if a gut punch was delivered to the back of my heart
from shame's curled up fist, infuriated at my procrastination.
Carotid artery did not see this coming.

Shame has a job to do, but then must be filtered out
though deliberate exhalations and breeze-blown prayers.

Today the tree is a wagon wheel-sized stump
sitting alongside the path I'm on,
like a reluctant and forlorn forest troll
that wouldn't hurt a fly.
It holds no bitterness toward the termites it hosts.

The sound of wind though its unfurled leaves
have left no memories,
like a vacant chair no one is certain
ever had a sitter,
but you could've sworn you'd once heard it creak under the weight
of someone.
Maybe yourself.

Maybe.

Postscript in the Past Perfect
Allen Braden

London. 1940. Bombers in formation
herd clouds before them like a cowcatcher.

But this is Tacoma. Present day. The air raid
siren just a shift change at Almond Roca.

It's only a fleet of geese flummoxed
by the exhaust from our pulp mills.

Instinct's a mystery. The magnetization
of migrant wishbones remains a code

unbroken. We're all survivors one way
or another. Our victory gardens were

tilled under for The Sound Garden.
Grunge now cleans up the airwaves.

See how easily the eye deceives?
Listen close & I'll show you.

Shakabrah Diner
Allen Braden

The group one booth over deliberates
what to visit in Vegas—a museum
for Liberace or Cold War nuclear testing.

Liberace's closes this spring, one points out.
I imagine the homeless of Nevada, at cross-
streets and off-ramps, bravoing and encoring

in sequined capes or glam-buckled, velvet
platform shoes. Come easy, go easy.
The diner hangs in there (from Susie Q.

to Chaka Kahn, Adam & Eve dished up
on a plate for our hunger. The front door
okayed for hippies and other subversives).

The beloved. The unloved. Here together,
ordering, slurping, arguing, eavesdropping.
Hipsters slouch in the back door nowadays.

Shame on my contemporary plainspoken
shoes. Shame on the whole milk explosion
in my espresso, so like a mushroom cloud.

(previously published in *20/20: Tacoma in Images and Verse*)

the mountain is bleeding out__
francis faye oak

i soak in a never-ending catastrophe
as a september drizzle pools
in the unfilled holes where
soil meets fresh concrete, &

every feeble attempt to hide
from the encroaching darkness falls flat
on the drenched landscape that dying
leaves scattered across my memory

i shiver with new cold returning
as if smelling death for the first time &
at last hear the parched creatures
begging for mercy

while white patriarchs devour green
remains & nothing ever seems to change
besides the unfamiliar patterns
of increasingly terrifying weather

through tears life is trans-
formed into an inexplicable joy here
inside the dying womb of a life-giving
planet i never chose for myself

i was born into this
for heaven's sake

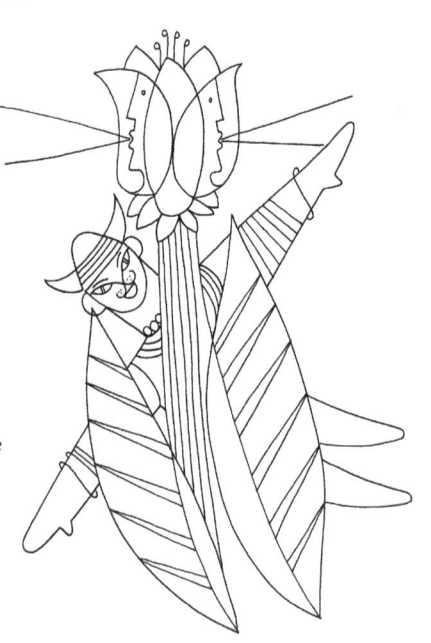

SONNET IV - A Graduation Sonnet
Claudia Riiff Finseth

I stand in swirling mist and sun of morning,
Your spirit in my hands. Coyote watches
From just behind the snowberry. Heron,
Wading in shallow water, turns an eye.
Beside me hovers blue-green dragonfly.
I feel their pulses keeping time with mine
And yours like beating drums. It's the world,
Calling you out, calling you on. Our breathing
Surges, and I fling you to the sky.
Your pinions spread, you catch the morning wind,
The sun glances off your wings as every instinct
Takes you up, and up, and ever up.
      Eagle is waiting for you, soaring high.
      I salute until you circle out of sight.

for Eric and Sarah on their high school graduations

Tacomaturity
Trevor Neil White

I never feel safer than when I'm walking home alone at night.
It's a privilege, admittedly,
but it's the only time I'm truly off the clock,
amid vacant architecture and uninquisitive dark.
For this, Tacoma's a sight more inviting in adulthood
than days I'd been by prior:
Fidgeting into existence at St. Joe's
or horizontal with a Hinge fling that went sideways,
the bawdy bodybuilder who made like pre-pandemic Covid
and distanced me.

Sure, there's some gutted storefronts, ill-advised alleys—
same as any burg—
but look past the liminal and the criminal,
and every neighborhood shouts its own song,
stitching a concrete quilt of community.

Take the busted piñata of Sixth Ave,
effusive murals crawling like iridescent ivy
over chipped-brick façades,
while I honor physical media's Holy Trinity
of Hi-Voltage, Stargazer, and Elegant Octopus
or mentally emit a post-college "YOLO"
over Red Bull in a bucket of booze
as Jazzbones' finest pay tribute to the classics.
Even if I can't pass for adolescent anymore,
youth is just a zip code away.

Now, not saying I didn't get out much before moving here
but, thirtysomething, I had to dip out of a dive bar on STW for an ATM
because I hadn't heard of a cover charge.
Now, though, I know those streets well:
Communion at Church Cantina,
that gorehound watering hole—shadowed respite
to alluring goths and skee-ball champs alike.
The Java Jive's effervescent kettle, brewing
a bill-spangled ceiling above a cavern of camaraderie.
Wrestlin' at Edison Square, a violent cabaret
within spitting distance of venues fit to ring your ears
as much as any bell.

It's a place of contradictions, like
the Dome in question, improbably ensconcing

jams of both the Monster and musical variety,
air thick with diesel one night and lyrics the next,
a modern coliseum beneath steel boughs.
Twilight mid-Rainiers game, tailgates radiating
as Cheney Stadium brings folks together
to cheer, jeer, or toast a beer.
Opulent Old Town, a humble cabin to one side
and six-figure vistas to the other.

Or, north, downtown:
The Convention Center, a rigid, reflective nexus
looming over the Port
and parking garages built like back-in Backrooms;
the Elks Temple, an ornate lasagna
of vintage kitsch and timeless class;
the Museum of Glass and its
conical monument to the curvaceous yet crystalline;
TAM's mass of canvasses and the tealit Brewery Blocks.
Even a staycation sunset, painting the Narrows a placid gold
or placing Tahoma on a pink-and-blue platter
astride my ashen balcony banister,
beats some trips I've taken abroad.

Stories tell you more about people than facts,
and this city's got plenty:
Jawless Jerry, may his mangled fangs rip in peace;
tales told by little libraries, those streetside novelist's hovels;
and the legend of the open parking spot on St. Helens Ave
(or maybe that's just me).
Across it all, I admire
Don't quit your night job, aspiring as I do
to the art-marketeers, the open-mic mavericks,
the burlesque girls and punk-rock royalty.
And so, eyes and ears popping
atop 1201 Pacific, it's a view to a skill:
Commencement Bay, indeed.
So many opportunities to be a moment
in someone's life or vice-versa.

From a certain perspective, it's all been downhill
ever since they stopped handing out safety scissors and glue in school.
I used to hope so much that
I thought imagination made me amazing,
but wanting's not a personality,
at least when I have the passions of a man
with half my sanity.
I think it all worked out, though,

because there's so much to *do* here.
I think this is where I finally have a chance
to be an urbane legend, refined in reverse
from plastic to oil, frivolity to energy,
trading two dimensions for true intentions.
No longer marooned on a kitchen island of idleness,
waiting for the right interlocking of ideas—
dreaming deep but thinking small—
I can resign from the pity party planning committee
and be a part of something:

A theater, say, stage or screen,
putting on a play for the ages at Pantages
or orchestrating the Sound's greatest film discussion
post-Oscar nom in The Grand
or something cheesy at Blue Mouse.
Writing, no matter the format:
prose, poetry, scripts, lyrics, anything
where what's meant matters more than what's said,
and what could be is more important than what is.
And though it's dead and gone, believe me—
ALMA's memory will carry on,
if not in a sick music venue
then in whatever clique I finally assemble
from guitarists, artists, sparring partners, and everyone else
who wants to *make*, not just *take*,
before we all trade headlines for headstones.

There's not a lot of traffic,
the inclines are great for legs day,
and when the clouds clear up,
I couldn't pick a better place to stroll with my backpack-bound cat
than Wright Park.
I just need one more walk home in the dark
to rehydrate, meditate,
check my schedule,
and then not just stand up
but finally wake up.

Chapter 4

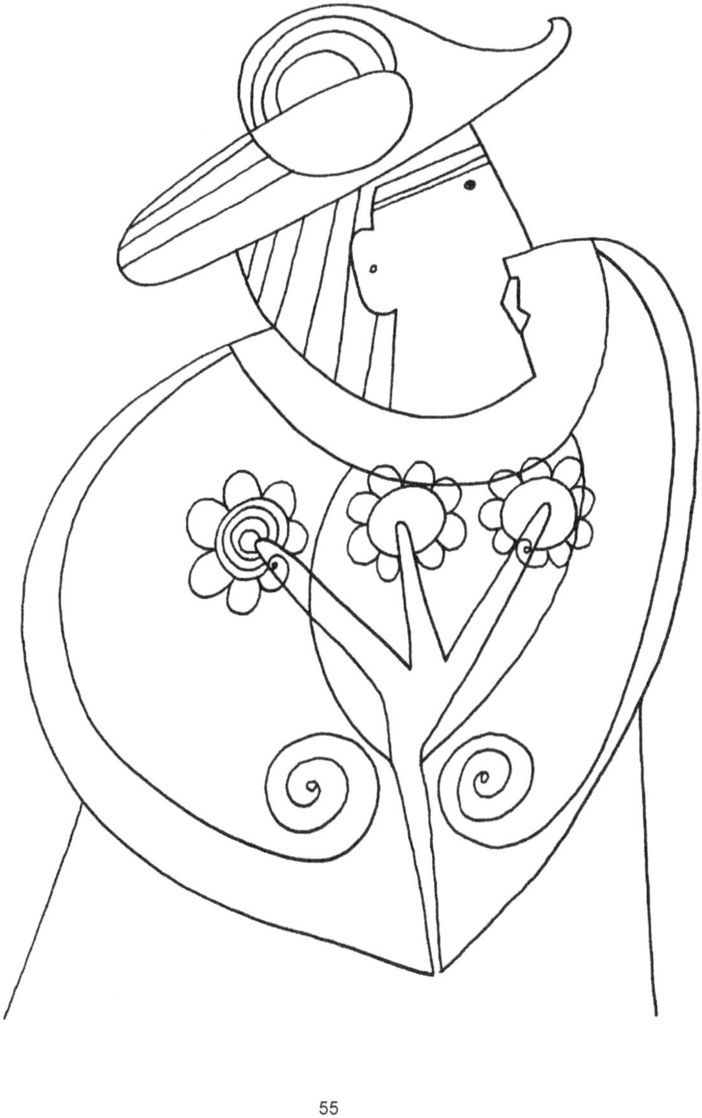

an ode to the stadium district:
Isaac Rodriguez

Rows and so many rows
Yards and dormers and gardens
an Idyllic heart with a lively pulse
The blood pumping through sounds like
a pretty brown girl walking a big white dog
the clang of the tracks as the train passes
A couple with entwined hands
Cross the street and
Green and so much green
Water and gravel and marble
The lungs filled with fresh air
The breath being drawn in sounds like
sylvan in the midst of brick and glass
the wonder of a child as they leave
the conservatory

The Way to Saint Pat
Emily Meyer

This yard is as far as I go into the church
The sun hit eastside like glass shards
Skipping downhill over treacherous cobblestone
Tripping me in confident distraction

Everyone I know exists in this square mile
I pass their houses with my head down, as if anyone looking
Could see the love, distaste, the longing
Faded under years of sure steps

Wherever I begin, I wind up here
Heedless of how the distance grows
Between home and my reflection
That, at least, changes slowly

```
                                                            E
                                                        E
    R                   G
        E           U
                F
```

N.L. Edwin

I

An unexpected
        addition to the kindergarten class
Modasir does not speak English
I thought it might be rude to assume
But my son and I said Salaam Alaikum
Instantaneously
        his face morphed before us
The distance
        in his eyes blinked away
And now he was there standing with us

II

Something that might be overlooked
Is the way refugees are talked to
By native English speakers
Talking loudly as if that will offer clarity
While asking pedantically, "Did you get that?"
Arriving here to escape war
Exhausted
They are cloaked geniuses

III

To the involuntarily untethered finding themselves here
        Hidden behind language barriers
        Searching for the feeling of safety
A city with publicly stated open arms
A city in the company of relatively not many
        Whispers gently
Welcome in
Welcome in
Welcome to a new home

IV

Tacoma
Welcoming City
Since 2014

Tacoma Rainbow
Gertrude Haley Bader

I saw a beautiful vision today!
A rainbow gleamed over Stadium Way.
It spanned the harbor from shore to shore,
Celestial omen of ancient lore.
In Stadium's fastness anchored deep,
Its spectrum colors formed to leap,
Then gird the sky to Dash Point's breast,
And there among the pine trees rest.

O I watched the vision with lifted eyes,
The pot of gold and the sailor's warning;
Rebirth of flowers in the skies,
Hope of the night, dread of the morning!
Search for the goldpot where you may,
Dig in the harbor or fathom the bay!

The Poetry of Gertrude Haley Bader, Pageant Press, Inc., 1961

Take a breath
Rebecca Amina Echeverria

for Linsey and all my mixed women

you caught my
sighs and they jumble tumbled
out
and fed them back/ground up to me
        spicy chicken
        lovely, folded
        into potsticker wraps

we are everything at once
and so, in their country/culture
nothin' much.

we are so far from packing
in boxes
that we walk our roads, light
packages piled from our crowns to the clouds.

there are many words for women like us
and they are not, um...flattering

so we grind up the definitions
between survival and exile
and make it a dialectic

fuck resilience, we dig with our hands

and find one another
    teeth glinting
as we dance huddled
to the dark pockets
of our/own cities

Delinquent
Tammy Robacker

                                                          [Sealed court proceedings
                                                          will be treated as though
                                                            they never took place.

                                                  *

Being a poor girl
was my first offense.
Lipstick secondary.

Pink Illusions—
I carried it out
in my fist.

                                                  *

*"If Bon Marche make us pay
for the stolen thingies,
we can have the jeans, no?"*

                        Asks my immigrant mom
                        while reading
                        the arrest paperwork.

                                                  *

"I do not know you anymore."

                        Says mother who praises Jesus from a sectional sofa
                        who sends our money away to The 700 Club on TV

                        Says father who buys me round-trip Greyhound tickets
                        who lets me visit him once a year every June for 10 days

                        Says me who wears Greatlash in very black
                        and Kotex with wings

                                                  *

Watch bubble mirror for narcs. Pocket blush. Slide liners up sleeve.
Go somewhere dead (like House/Home). Drop all empty packaging.

*

                Two detached parents
                like warm, fleshy lobes
                to push safety pins through

                Flared nostril
                Furrowed brow
                Flipped lip

                Control is the hole
                I punch
                inside of you

*

Personal belongings: Purse
Style: Clutch
Contents: Purple Rain nail polish
cut price tags lip gloss three bucks
bus transfer four plastic sacks key
Note: No parent available by phone

*

                              If someone asks about your sealed file,
                                      the law requires the answer,
                              "We have no records of that matter."]

Beyond This Violet Fabric
Sandra K. King

Today, the wake on Lake Michigan's shore
through sun-squint view
looks the same as that of Puget Sound,

but one is fresh water,
the other, salty like
blood

which I am told is thicker
than the waters of
either.

I tend to agree
with this saying
most of the time.

The sand on this beach is composed of
full-circle particles—
silica and oxygen,

chaos of quartz semi-orbs and
smashed shards of spheres
like mini mute crystal balls

which shuffle nervously underfoot
and inaudibly whisper about past sins and the secrets
of my future.

Family is gathered at lakeside lodge further inland
and if it's possible to fill a gene pool with tears
I am drowning in it.

Last night's rainless storm
brought conflict
of air masses.

Stark realities of shocking duplicity
were broken cymbals in the clumsy hands
of time stumbling on, undaunted,

despite its rhythm nearly tripped up by
human failing. So many reasons
to weep.

We bury our dead,
dust off our shoes and stare at ceilings
under protective roofs,

say our prayers and swear to God
we can see right through overhead opacity
to distant unfurling purple cloud cover.

Somewhere beyond this violet fabric
wayward lightning bolts, rogue and unbridled,
tear through galactic garment of stars.

This is the same shimmering host
which looks down over my home thousands
of miles away

where a beloved who'd once secretly
planted flowers in our yard
now sets them ablaze.

Who can sleep through the roar of flames,
hollow echoes from light years away,
the gasping rales of a million dying suns?

What heart can resist
succumbing to obliteration
from such mournful metaphysics?

Oblivious daybreak
carves gashes
through swollen eyelids

which brings to awareness that,
at least for the hovering gulls
it's business as usual though,

and the surf's rhythm on any given shore
remains resilient
and relentless.

Be Gay, Do Crime
Vaquero Azul

"It's everywhere" i whisper
As a white person across the room
Complains of what's happening, "Too much, all the time, too soon"
You tell your friend "The grass is greener on the other side! If I fled to another country, it's better, it's safer.We need to hide."
Why do the white gays always want to flee first?
Why do brown gays have to hold it down?
What happened to "We have to dismantle the system together"
What happened to "Be Gay, Do Crime?"
Fleeing won't solve anything
"It's everywhere" I lock them in the eyes.
"Racism, Colorism, Transphobia, Homophobia, Genocide."
"If you flee to another country, will you get to know the people, will you see what ails them? Will you fight for the marginalized?"

Or will you treat it like a vacationer in Hawaii... a guest... will you wrap yourself in the local food.. the scenery...a blanket of cozy ignorance... Play tourist for the rest of your life?

Or will you let the flames of anger lick your face? Will you let the grief arm you? To pick up the mantle and fight? To bring community to others?
To give land back to the Indigenous.
To boycott companies and never condone Genocide.

Free Palenstine, Free Congo, Free Sudan, Black Lives Matter, LGBT Lives Matter, Trans Lives Matter, Asian Lives Matter, Land Back, Land Back to Hawaii & Puerto Rico, Fight for Missing and Murdered Indigenous Women.

Dig your feet into the soil you're on right this moment
And
Fight"

My Story Mixed
Jack Morrow

The special thing about me
is that I wasn't born here,
I was born in Alaska.
I was in Alaska for six months only,
I'm now seven in Tacoma and

It's been a pain at school with the bullies and enemies,
but think about Tacoma as school
when you were young
and how it was hard for you
and think about what you would do.
Would you take a deep breath? or go to a calm space?
And that decision is up to you,
don't underestimate the way that you want to do it.
We all think differently, and that's what special about everyone,
and I feel like that's awesome!!

at the point of defiance__
francis faye oak

i rise alone, with a corrosive emptiness
cascading over me in alkaline baths
of dread and self-doubt

& yesterday's euphoria rippling
into continents of self-betrayal
that divide an ocean of soul

into traumatic landscapes
& necessary desolations
of barren sounds & prickly thorns

with a silent voice whispering and poking
incessantly posing the most alluring of lies:
don't you think you've already gone far enough
_____

i stretch beyond, a skeleton draped
in sparkles sashaying into
the singeing depths of conformity

moving into the flames of a culture of mistaken identities, fooled
fools fueled by manipulated desires

every movement giving way
to tiny deaths, *la petite mort,*
earth-rattling sensations unraveling

a body mummified
for forty years

Nothing & Everything
Julie Van

We are all-you-can-eat people.
Love, a karaoke duet. Childhood
tasted like crinkle potato chips and clam
dip. I still smell the pickle juice on
dad's clothes, and I think a lot about
what my ancestors must think of me.

My third grade teacher dropped me off
and my mom had a laundry basket on her hip
in the parking lot. I hid my dad's cigarettes
in the glove compartment. I had always
thought I could change our stars.

The fading photographs
from when my parents got married
here, in this tiny living room with the shagged carpet
barely enough but just enough,
this American Dream of theirs.
Did I mean to say ours?

In between the sad lives and the mad lives,
Dr. Phil's voice bellows on the television
and three in the afternoon is lonely.
Five two-dollar bills for good luck,
three jobs with four kids for good measure.
I ache for the ghost of my mom at eighteen
labeled: *the day I left my country.*
Freedom has a foreign face. Showing up
in the cafetorium alone, I watch my own eyes

splitting white light into sunlight.
The least I could do
was swallow away my longing.
Only ever good for eating or talking,
my mother reminds me of the debts
we pay for a hungry mouth.

Long Live the Kingdom of Front Yardia, Realm Madison Street
Chloe Mohs

There's a tree on the slope of a yard I call home.
Carrying a branch bent from little hands hanging,
with a blistered grip.
Worn bark along its length,
and a few rusted nails lodged in the trunk from Halloweens past.

The grass beneath stays green the longest,
in the summertime.
Before watering was given up and it took brown, left to die.
Shade is a blessing in the dry heat of July in
Tacoma.

Before the time where a tree is only a tree,
summer vision made hazy the reality of life.
The breeze replaced our AC,
and the birds became our symphony.
Dreams leaked from between our hands, slipping through in golden threads,
weaving out our domain.

Upon withering moss, beneath blue sky,
the turquoise blanket we spread, laid forth the kingdom,
made of roly polys and the dogs who passed by.
We plucked maple leaves and ground them between our fingers,
until the green rubbed onto skin in a guileless dye.

We took the pieces and dropped them into our soap and dandelion "perfume,"
fit for the kings and queens of Madison Street.
White Clover adorned our hair. California Poppy tucked behind our ears.
We were knights in shining sun hats to the worms caught on the hot cement.

We'd climb high and touch the sun,
look out over the land and yell "we can see the house from here!"
Innocent in our conquest; pure in intent.
We were anything and everything we could imagine at the top of the world,
screaming our swan song of
childhood.

Chapter 5

in Tacoma
Sarah Heavin

I lived
in Tacoma
when I started my adult life.
At first
this place was

    unwanted

House rented
Sight unseen
Because why

    Tacoma?

Give it a year, I said
Maybe it'll be better
than what Seattle says about it

I arrived in Stadium District
Rankos on the corner
the morning summer light

A drive on 6th Ave
an e9 pizza
A beer at the corner bar

    hopeful

That maybe
this place was

    More.

I became a professional
in Tacoma
The UPS campus
Perfectly groomed
The sounds of students
Rushing
Thinking
Doing

    Learning.

I became a mother

in Tacoma
Pushing babies out in the same

    alien tower

where all Tacomans
push out their babies.

Strollers in wright park
Itchy shins from brackish water
Gingerbread houses at Murano
Money passing hands at teaching toys
Sticky fingers at frisko freeze
Because the soft serve is

    Dripping

I learned to love Tacoma
Monkeyshines
Beautiful Angle
Walks all over town
the secret smile of knowing that we are

    Hunting
    Together.

I lost my first "love"
in Tacoma.
After pushing the baby out in the alien tower
His love left
Maybe

    Sneaking out

the strange shaped window
Or maybe it was lost
somewhere else

The 11th street bridge
The viewing tower
Opera alley

Places that should have romance
But didn't
Not for us.

I was betrayed
in Tacoma
The realization came at Alma
Music loud
Tacomans dancing
Tacomans loving
And me
    Alone

While the "man" who watched
me push out the baby and wipe the sticky fingers

Now watched
Someone else
Someone I thought was a
    "Friend."

And then I thought

"My only friend is Tacoma"

But it wasn't
    All of Tacoma was my friend.

Because this is a
small town
with a

    Long
    Memory

I found comfort
in Tacoma
Walks everywhere
Tears spilled
More tears than the rain

Tears
In Tacoma
Tears at
viet dong
Tacos y maricosa
Port roads
Stadium High School
South Tacoma Way
Curran Coffee
Jack Hyde

Tears spilled
all
over
this
town
I found love
in Tacoma
At Bar Rosa
A sunny day Tuesday in May
I was swiping for fun
and found
    More.

And now I am

In love
In Tacoma
Every street now looks
Like it is breathing
Like the city is

Pulsing
Pulling
Pumping
Pushing

My broken heart
Back
Into
    One Piece

And now I am

    In Peace

In Tacoma

Because

    Tacoma is for Lovers.

Hilltop Musings
Joshua Olver

Hilltop, Hilltop
Tacoma neighborhood
Notorious and Beautiful
In the early morning golden hour
When the sky is pink
I saw you for the first time
The mountains were arrow heads
Buried in the sky
Her sidewalks naked
Except for broken glass infant of old buildings
She'd been left to dangle by mini Reagans
Who didn't see her beauty or feel her worth
Sirens scream
Alarms echo through parking garages
In her morning is a melody
Hilltop, Hilltop
Her melody will rush all through you
When the sun kisses those brick buildings
Her charms cannot be so easily faded out
That slick 70's glance
Black Wall Street swing in your stride
Now they say they want to
"Bring life back to Hilltop"
As if they could bring more life to you
Hilltop, Hilltop
I love you
I was never yours for good
But without you things would have been a lot worse

Sequoia in the City
Phil Harty

Dry ground round
the base of a Giant Sequoia
Laze on a bed
Of shed burnt orange
withering foliage

Burgeoning streets encircle
Walkers ramble as cars rumble
with whirring wheels spinning
all passing with perpetual pace

Crows cackle and swoop
On damp grass with gimpy gait
Poking through leaf litter
As I'm snug against the colossal tree

I gather and release each breath
Circulation taps into depths head to toe
Roots are a conduit pathway
To the tip of the conifer cone

A soft wood cinnamon brown
From top of tall crown down
An annual blue green fibrous gown
A buffer from bitter weather temperaments

Searching has led me to stray
In the city where Sequoia sways
A place to listen in stillness to solace

Chickadees melodious chatter resounds
All throughout the canopy
With wind commotion curtailed
As acrobats they bound through interlaced branches

Looking at an old leafless Tulip tree
Skeletal branches sprawled to sky
Limbs with fractal fingers
Golden sapphire fiery glow
Of setting Sun seeps thru
Cracks of lavender-grey clouds

My eyes rise leisurely
branches spiral upward
from a towering and gnarled tree trunk
I stretch my spine in mimicry

Learn.
Xandra Egge

I saw the blue mountain laughing down at us
As we walked it shorts by the water.
It wasn't kind and it wasn't cruel,
But it was clear, and made the day seem hotter.

And we wanted to know many things.
How to be still.
And how to give grace,
How to stand firm
With the wind in our face.

It wasn't kind and it wasn't cruel,
It was just a matter of fact
That as we walked in thought by the water,
The mountain had knowledge we lacked.

And it tried to teach us many things.
How to rest calmly
And put worry away.
How to hear the song
Of the trees as they sway.

Away from Home
Felicia Tran

I dream, I dream
Patience accompanies me on the railways
Snoozy, sleepy, asleep

I forget the healing balm the salve
Of the salty air, of the salty sea winds

But as I went elsewhere,
I realized this was my home.
Here, healing did its work
even while here continued to break me down.

Always broken
Always mending
I sought the curses of my persistent torment
But alas, when I return home,
I am empty handed.
No answers, no solutions.

Certain lands, certain airs
Hold what I need to exist a little stronger
But my heart is not settled
And so I continue to bear the burns, the tears, the rips, the stings, the aches, the tenderness
Until I've had my share, and then,
And then,
I make the choice, again,
To call here, home.

KIA Boys are loose
Thomas Nolan

Skittering about like a mad mouse
The KIA Boys are on the loose
They're sporting guns in T-town
And thinking they're invincible
It's just a game to steal a car
And rev it into the ultra wild
The KIA Boys are up to no good
Connoisseurs of mayhem
Game's over fellas
You've threatened the last life
Handcuffed and detected
Their last ride was demented
On through the park
And dark and into the drink
You've reached the duck pond
And now it's time to sink
Go now and take your punishment
It's a slick way to spend the holiday
Tell your pals in the Air Jordans
That the last splash was not a gas
Into the murky night you'll go
In shiny handcuffs Geronimo

Dawn in Tacoma
Tia Pliskow

I encompass 219,000 dreams,
My dome a blue-rayed sun
Rising in the east.
The backdrop a mountain
Named by the Salish People
The Mother of the city.

What's the Destiny of the City of Destiny?
Allen Braden

It's like an Appaloosa without pants,
        seemingly as natural as Wright Park.
Like Almond Roca except without
        the nuts and *sans* roca.
Like closed captions translating
        "performance poetry"
        as "foreign policy"
        or "came to Tacoma"
        as "Cuban lymphoma."
Like a grove of beige condos sprawling.
Like Costco and REI book-ending our first
        cemetery in the city limits.
Like the Union Pacific stopping
        at Titlow for ice cream.
Like the Rendering Plant reminder:
        Holstein, Brown Swiss and Charolais
        gave their milk a lifetime ago.
Like the octopus under Narrows Bridge,
        grown so massive it couldn't surface
        even if it wanted to.

The Point Obscured
Emily Meyer

Mist swallows the sound
carried on waves unseen
Along tides that etched eons
and now lap gently at your sneakers

As you stand
submerged in a cloud
Salt on throat and tongue
And all around, water

Icarus in transit
Albert de Santis

A young boy with breasts
questionably dressed
in halter-top in cream
and sandals and cut-off jeans
all dangly with frays
was left like a stray
on the fifteenth corner
of Tacoma Avenue

the possible fledge
unburdens the red
pickup truck bed
of his belongings
bulging in green
garbage bags

The boy rages
at the middle aged
man in the driver's seat
whose gaunt neck twists
in collared shirt
directs plastic black
sunglasses at me

The man pulls out
distancing himself
from the boy's
rigid middle digit
and turns up Fifteenth.

I turn too
downhill to 705
unwitting witness
during my last mile
in a Brugel Tacoma

Zooming Through
David Gilmour

Black-backed gull, animate as old King Raven,
I zoom away on broad Commencement Bay
Over by steep Point Defiance clay palisades
Where we dip and rise, swoop and slurp,
Rising and falling on balls of herring hatch,
Screaming and wailing in festival gluttony.

Onward I swerve past the tideline, Katie Downs,
Harbor Lights, veering to snag some offal treat,
Past gray, mothballed war ships, vacated, stiff,
Moored close to shore by the Schuster Parkway.
My cormorant kin, squads of slim silhouettes
Line the hawsers, dark divers ready to launch
After airing their wings, balanced, noble, erect.

Onward through the cage of the 11th Street Bridge,
Named for Murray Morgan, famed writer historian.
Bridge lifter and resident once, Tacoma his home.
Then Fosse, cleansed of bilge silt at great expense, and
Whoa! What a span, the glistening lines, a winged ship
My ilk in cables, the 509, nighttime diamonds and all.

Beyond is the Dome, a place for my rest, a great gray head,
Decorated in Argyle sock, as if triangles are in fashion.
That's where I stand and ponder beyond, the great white
Mother of Tahoma fame, ponderous rock of frozen heights.
White robed Mount Tahoma, my cousin Raven's haunts,
Who does not fear to wander our Commencement Bay,
Leaving the Lushootseed lands to regenerate green trees
And spawn in River of Salmon to make way in wild rutting.
For us there is plenty together in the sweet city of Destiny.

you'll love, tacoma__
francis faye oak

come live in a city
of forgotten kids, stuck
out in the middle of nowhere,

perfectly designed for us
not to think at all about the source
of our ignorance, nor the price
of cheapening good

_____

dawn rises to another red sun
shrouded in an acrid haze turning
the horizon yellow & blurry,

demonstrated proof of the disastrous living
conditions that we attempt to normalize
by going to the beach & pretending
our lungs aren't burning

with numbed senses we bury
our minds in the sand like
forgotten artifacts whose pricelessness
makes them easy targets
for ongoing speculation

our soft bodies splayed open &
vulnerable, like sacred land devoured
by a contagion that infects the heart
of what it means to be alive
without acknowledgment

we lie around & watch as poisonous
clouds tiptoe above a shaking foundation,
until the hills dissolve into dusty desolations
with sunburnt skin & a deep voice
warning the news is getting worse

_____

it's an admittedly queer
setting for a love story

S 74th to N 33rd on the Tree Street
Erik Hanberg

Oakes, Pine, Cedar, Alder
One street, yet four trees
A whole forest from one trunk
Swaying east and west
Tacoma's contoured spine

Hearty thick oakes
Strong enough to hold up Tacoma
(Though we test it too often)
Strong enough for the other trees
Strong enough for that extra vowel

At the mall, the pine is grafted on
It's evergreen, like the post office
Evergreen, to filter the air
From the foundries and pulp mills
It saws through in the Valley

Smell the pungent cedar bark
As you dip under sixteen
Come visit the scenic back doors
Of Walmart, hospitals, condos
Elks, grazing in their enclosure

Then the alder, a pioneer species
Alone on the peninsula?
The only N branch
Where its drivers like to pretend
That the trees stops at sixth

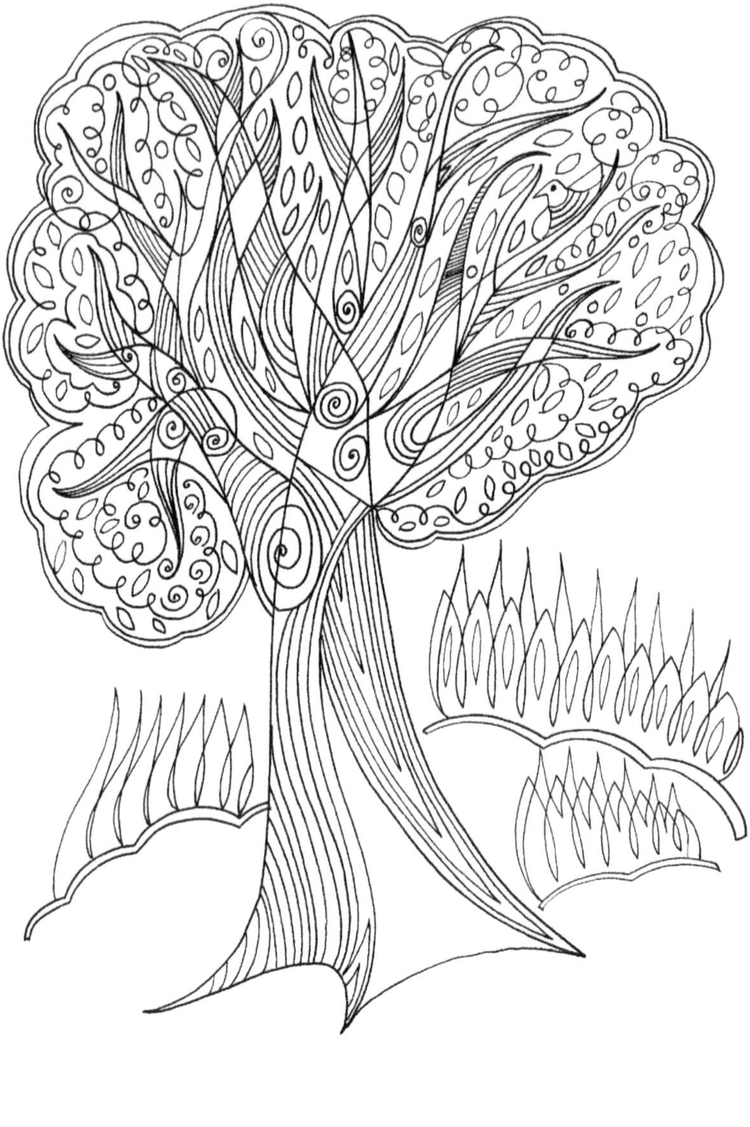

ii
Yuri Arakaki

some safe haven
we no longer can carry anger in
the way we did as kids.
there are always butterflies when you're near
and i named one "reasons"
to live and let go of all the things
you cannot control; you noticed
what you've always hated
so beautifully captured and
taken with ice in front of you
and suddenly feel so okay with
the sun that gets let in,
that deep-set color
forces of nature paint you in–
somehow and somewhere
perpetual motion makes a still beauty
feel less alone in a world where
they've learned loneliness is
a constant symptom in always moving
or not moving at all.

Douche Bag
Sam Cori

Douche bag,
Do you miss what we had?
And the trouble we'd get into

Every morning
doing the
thing you
like to
do and
don't you
know i
like it
too?

Douche Bag,
Oh.
Remembering what we had...

A thousand promises
accompanied
a thousand of your kisses

        But you broke 'em
        like you broke me.

Hey.

Douche Bag...
Number one douche bag.
My Favorite Douche Bag.

The way you rock your blue jeans,
Your backwards hat and cigarette, it means.. You're from Tacoma, Washington
and like to have-a too much fun

And it
Really.
Drives me
Wild.

Yeah.
Douche Bag.

We would be rock steady
If you'd learn to come and get me
I just wanna be your lady
          I'd be the first fucking lady of the Douche Bag Committee.
You had me slowly and completely,
Yeah, you gave it to me sweetly
If your friends all knew who I was
Yeah, they'd really wanna meet me.

But you hide me in your mailbox,
Where you keep all of your feelings
You say you're a real Douche Bag
But to me, you're just
a real
a-fuckin
sweetie.
Douche Bag you're glad to meet me.

Yeah, douche bag.
My favorite douche bag.

Douche Bag
Remembering what we had..
Makes me want to claw right through the concrete just to get closer to your street.
I want to be really bad

Just not as bad as you.
Yeah, do whatever the fuck you wanna do. My favorite douche bag,
You made me mean mad.

And I know you really wanna get some. Babe,
But I'm Tacoma Wholesome
And I want more than just your bed
You bad bad American Douche Bag.

Chapter 6

one account of provenance-1
John Sexton

children of the train, lincoln's signature, all those japanese hands – cast out!
destiny which is unevenly accorded.

children of western expansion, of a doctrine
called supreme. children of lands parceled and desecrated, economized as a topography
of casinos and the weyerhaeuser corporation

children of increasing speed

children of hope and of jealous expulsion,
children of greed and of a faith which only proved superficial, only ever
until the next big thing.

children of the strata, learned to distinguish
          our kind from others. children of the drawn lips and tight nod.

yet all of us arrived homeless
and stumbling,
making our case against the thumb on the scale in the great lottery of the city.
its
jagged shape

cresting the hill, ascending, ascending! or else– tumbling into frigid wake.

Propitious
St. Rita's Catholic Church, Ainsworth Ave, Tacoma
Jessika Satori

We gather, every Saturday morning at 9am
to pray to and for St. Rita's.
"Be propitious to us, St. Rita!"

The multi-generational Italian families, who
built and prayed,
married and stayed,
in Tacoma to grow their families.

St. Benedict prays on the left,
St. Rita, watches on the right,
and Jesus is in the middle,
always in the center,
the reason why we are here.

St. Rita's Church stands on the corner of Compassion and Care.
and even though some forces don't want her there,
There are others who hold her close,
the live ones who meet, and the ghosts
of loved ones who live within the walls.
And in the gold-glowing morning, we are all called.

Breakfast Burrito
B. Eugene B.

There she sits
Astride South End's natural speed bump
(A crest of the road at 72nd & Park).

Many will miss her
(Oh, a misfortunate for them)
As their gaze follows, in cadence, high-voltage transmission lines
Rising & falling, westward toward Winco,
Eastward toward Pacific Ave. & beyond.

She sits snug; low & rectangular,
Her canopy jutting out as a gaping jaw
Preparing to ruminate
Plastic picnic tables in the shade.
Flaunting a broad tangerine-pink accent
Flamed across her tawny-yellow brick front.

A lullaby
In stenciled letters
Along the top of the wall
The specialities of TAQUERIA EL GRANDE

(MO)JARRA FRITA   TORTAS   QUESADILLAS   TACOS   BREAKFAST BURRITOS

In letters like ants
Marching along the rim of her hat.

Slow down the next time you pass by
                    Embrace her beauty & listen to her cry.

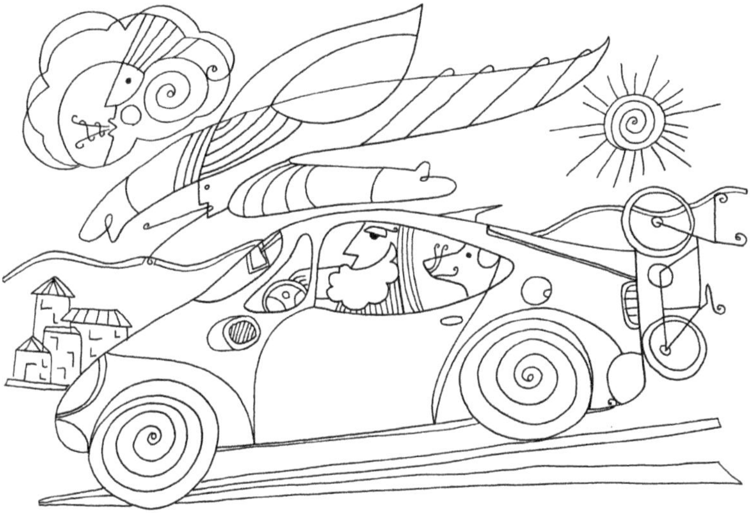

The Hilltop Heartbreak
Karen Cruz

It's been two months
since I made my way northwest,
to the city tucked beside the bay.
Those back home begged me not to leave,
warning that come winter
I'd miss the sun.
I have only a season
before I find out.
We're currently in
the belly of August,
swamped in triple digit heat,
the sun baking the city murals
like colorful cookies.
The summer's here
to wring us all dry.

The brick building I live in
is slumped and crumbling
amidst the new builds.
I respect the stubbornness.
The hardwoods complain
whenever I walk on them,
and there's a kitchen
I can sidle into.
Not like the kitchen we had
when we were married,
where two could tango.
A TV shares my sleeping spot
on the floor, unplugged and unmotivated.
We both aren't quite up to our tasks yet.

The heat is most persistent at night,
wafting through the window on
the salty breath of the Sound,
humid in my lungs
while I gaze at the ceiling
and count the cranes.
It raises memories
like a necromancer,
ghosts of our old life
in the desert-

the mornings you spent whistling
over chorizo and eggs
while the cat purred beside me-

sharing a warm Corona on the balcony
while we read our books-

snow fluttering onto our yard,
salting the Christmas lights.

Your leather jackets,
and comma smile.

We were so young,
and it felt safe and natural
to plant ourselves
in the soil of one another,
a soil we hoped
even the desert wouldn't wither.
But now I am alone, in a city by the bay,
melting like a candle in that unforgiving heat,
burning and settling
into a different singed shape each day.
Some days sharp and despairing,
other days round and receptive.
I am hopelessly awake with ragged eyes
while the trains chant by the waterfront,
and the seagulls blare through black smoke stacks,
and the sun never felt
further away.
I am lying in the bed I've made.

The ceiling turns blurry,
the sheets damp on my neck,
the fan spinning
with a hypnotizing click.
If someone shook me
they'd hear the broken pieces
rattling around inside.

Cheer up, I tell myself in the dark,
throat tensed and burning.
Tomorrow
the mountain
will come out.

But the tears come regardless,
and the ache is almost unbearable,

because I know

you would've loved it
here.

Suspension
Melody Derrick

On film, the roadbed
crumbles like sand around a fossil.
It does not show the long decade
until fat America, postwar flush,
rebuilt it. And then another.
Under perfect mammoth tusks,
slick grates scatter those winds,
crisp white signs command order.
I purse my lips at the lanechangers,
their disrespect.
The bridge closes my eyes,
suspends my spine in the split seconds
before solid ground,
and again
in the mirror,
a grainy frame,
a flicker of a memory not my own.

Liquid Dream's
Susan Harmon

Whistle seeps into
My ears
Echos in my body
I feel the train
Singing in my bones
Keeping me
At arms length
From sleep
But not from dreams
Traveling with horses
My heart gallops
My body remembers
Times
Of iron wheels
Galloping into yesteryear
Water and drums
Silent sounds
Clash in the
Lightning streaked darkness
Sounds of war
And peace fill
My dreams and memories of
Sleeping
In your arms
I awake sweating
And alone

The Donna of Destiny
Jessica J. Bloodsaw

I am the donna of Tacoma.

Because I know my boundaries,
because Tacoma has always
been my address, I've seen
the many faces of Mount Rainier,
a different cheek
if you are in Tacoma proper
or improper,
I am the Donna.

Because I travel to the Tribes,
play their games and
seek their wonders, eat their fry
bread and drink freely
from other-worldly waters,
I am the Donna.

Because I have blood-rights,
because I grew up by the Base,
close enough to hear and feel
bombastic maneuvers, yet far
enough away to miss the sounds
of Revery and Retreat,
I am the Donna.

Because I never left,
and when I did, I came back
for my claim, my rights, my kin,
my blood bleeds forever free here
in the freest you can be in America,
without being an ex-pat Papa said,
I am the Donna.

Because of my legacy, my legends,
the stories told of my past,
my honors, royal lineage
in the great lake waters
on the furthest reaches
of the property lines,
I am the Donna.

Because I was fenced in,
cut down, reduced, reused,
recycled, reborn
from the city of destitute
into the City of Destiny;

I am the donna of Tacoma.

What sounds like rain
Meredith Smith

What sounds like rain
  is the pitter patter
  of sail ropes
  and tarps
  rippling against hulls
  in the boatyard

Migrant's Vade Mecum
Kristy Gledhill

To arrive and be of it, to ask a place to be your
new one, learn to speak it. Start with the primal

element. Go to the rock and gem show, sweltering
parking lot, east county, ringed with dusty RVs, tents

and tables, bins, buckets, boxes of rocks, pro-grade
rumbling rock polishers. Say the rock names out loud,

eavesdrop on the crusty old bolo-ed rockhounds
comparing their hauls, guarding their secret grounds,

strike up a conversation with the "retired U-Dub geo prof!"
giving away agates and mini vulcanology lectures to anyone

who'll listen. Listen. Handle the rocks, rub your sweaty
thumb into them as he tells you about Tahoma, Nisqually,

Cascadia subduction. Try not to worry. Try not to think of
Puget Sound as a Great Lake. Try not to ask about Petoskeys.

Ask instead about glaciers, their paths, the scars, the till.
Say "estuary." Ask for a map. Ask for a tide table. Ask how

you're supposed to get used to this ancient lava flow
under your feet, that serrated horizon, the way there's

no way to see what's coming at you with all these hills
and gulches and the firs, everywhere. Take the *Field*

Guide to Rocks of Washington he offers. Study it. Read it
out loud. Let the phrases wear a runnel of belonging into

your accreting memories, your speech, your belief that this
new place will have you, that you can, one day, be of it.

Sidewalk Poetry
Jessica Stovall

Waves sloshing (hush, hush)
Evergreen island
Shallow, spiraling verses embellishing wet concrete
Low timber rail; shells and stones left as offerings along its narrow horizon
Gulls calling (harsh, harsh)
Into the salty brine of the rain-fresh air
Damp fallen leaves
Small puddles soaking soggy sneakers
Grey path sandwiched between woods and water
Driftwood trees washed beyond the reach of the tide, rocks intermingled with tendriled roots
Wonder, greedy wonder -
Snapping picture after picture to preserve each poem like licking a melting ice cream cone
Another and another and another

City of Destiny, City of Shame
Jacque Lynn Schultz

As I sit alone, I shiver
Watching boats on Commencement Bay.
I'm visited by two hundred ghosts
Of those driven out one brutal day.

After building the Northern Pacific,
At its terminus, they chose to stay.
Building lives in Little Canton,
To remind them of their homes so far away.

Some owned shops, some had restaurants
Others logged, fished or mined.
These Chinese souls, mostly men,
Better workers you'd be hard-pressed to find.

Tacoma, City of Destiny
Tacoma, City of Shame
Tacoma, how could you run them out
Just because they didn't look the same

Be gone by the first of November,
the Mayor's edict read;
and in fear of what was to follow,
Two thirds of those Chinese fled.

As day dawned on the third of November,
At least two hundred had stayed.
All remaining driven from their homes,
Marched to a station seven miles away.

They were put on the train to Portland
and told never to return.
To ensure that was what happened,
Two days hence, Little Canton burned.

The Tacoma Method was highly praised
In papers near and far.
Twenty-seven white men arrested,
All released, lauded as stars.

This park of Reconciliation
Keeps the story alive,
So other generations won't forget
What happened back in 1885.

Tacoma, City of Destiny,
Tacoma, City of Shame,
Tacoma, how could you run them out
Just because they didn't look the same?
We ran them out
Because they did not look the same.

Note: It took the Tacoma City Council 122 years to approve a resolution to acknowledge that the 1885 expulsion was "a reprehensible occurrence" and another 18 years to open The Tacoma Chinese Reconciliation Park.

Poem in Which the Limits of a Gift Are Identified
Abby E. Murray

The gift doesn't begin with my neighbor
but the poem does, noting how he lumbers
from his front step to mine, walking
the way bears do on hind legs, as if always
reaching into trees that grow no arthritis
or old age or bum knees, as if searching
for only as much sweetness as they need.
The gift is a pineapple swaddled like Jesus
in a plastic Walmart bag, which my neighbor
carries in the crook of his flannel arm,
and when my doorbell rings, a strange new star
blinks awake in the sky. Here is the door
as I open it, which only means *I am here*,
which is a small thing but also everything,
and here are my neighbor's hands,
gnarled from decades of crawling under
other people's houses to heal busted pipes
and water heaters while the guts of his own
house corroded and split. He unbundles
the pineapple, which is an even bronze-gold
all over, not a bruise or blotch of green on it,
it is so perfect even I can tell, and I know
nothing about pineapples or even perfection,
really. *Struck it rich at the food bank today*,
my neighbor says, *thought I'd share*. And the gift
doesn't end there with the pineapple passed
to me or even in my kitchen where I carve it
a short while later, separating sunlight from
the prickly bark it has needed until now,

and it doesn't end in my daughter's mouth
or belly when she tastes it either, not even
when her lips form the words *thank you*
in response to my giving her this wealth to eat,
which was given to me, which was given
to my neighbor, given to an empty shelf,
given to a grocery store and before that
a truck, given the sky above dirt, given to dirt—
an experience we all have in common eventually,
givers and pineapples alike. And the gift
doesn't end with the bread I create by mixing
yeast with sugar, flour with water and salt and oil,
plus the two hours I borrow from my own sleep
then put in the oven to bake for my neighbor,
and to be honest, I'm sorry, I can't say where
these riches will end, ever, because I don't know.
I am here, like you, to open doors, accept
pineapples, share what I get, make bread
to wrap in a kitchen towel, ring doorbells,
extend my hands, and say *thank you*.

[original poem, unpublished, written about my neighborhood just off 6th Ave.]

Outside Marcia's Silver Spoon
Albert de Santis

My stolen kiss lays unrequited
on her small wet face, upturned
rain scooped by her white hood
overflowing hair akimbo
like a porcelain soup bowl
of broken ramen noodles
flecked by tumbling globs of water
her boots greyed in sintered clay
stomp the deepest puddle at me
into soggy puzzle pieces they splash
magically straight upward
and crash straight down
into her sky blue uppers
scurry on dirty rubber toes
flood upon her multivalent soles
rivulets down her unfastened collar
her boots like rain barrels
slosh as she stomps and squeals
back to the red Outback
'and it's time to go'
i laugh to myself, unfazed
next to the offending puddle
dry and warm i take my time
to unlock the car door for her
next year I'll start a new job
and we'll sell our Southend single-paned
home and leave Tacoma for good
and already I know, like a moment
that returns in a dream, this one
will return to me.

Chapter 7

In the beginning
Alexa Hoggatt

I
In the beginning

there was this:
Wild expanse of earth and sky
running into the sea

The sun on the surface
and the heat in the sand

the evergreens
in the small park by the hill

where we'd sit on the swings and know:
we were of this place
and it was enough

II
There was Tacoma

Such gold, such green and gray
such a bright shade of alive!

In the beginning there was only me
but for a moment there was *us*.

III
Then there was everything

Our world is too fragile to hold
steady now, our teachers whispered

*but steadiness is a myth from old stories
our parents told us to settle us to sleep and we've been sleeping
far too long.*

Midnight over and over
neon glow of the funeral home sign
across the street and the hotel rattling
with the strain of the heater

wasn't it lovely
not knowing where we'd wake up in the morning?
Wasn't it
akin to a promise?

Ivan
John Lawrence

They buried your thick bones
At Mountain View.
An unmarked grave, wet and shallow.
That's what creatures like us get.

You had a name
And still the ground lies
Putrid mud above you.

And yet I envy you,
For you gripped the cold steel
Of your cage.
And now the soft earth holds you,
Forgotten wretch.

My tomb is cold glass and as
I shriek the walls move
Ever inward.

I pace my tiny plot,
Children pass,
They point and ask,
"Mother what is that?"
"A monster."

My bones grow thick.

You Can Go Anywhere
John Kulm

You can go anywhere in Tacoma from East 38th.

Downtown? Turn north onto Pacific and keep going.

The windows of the high-rise condos on the waterfront are lit up and you can imagine living there.

The zoo at Point Defiance? Take the I-5 ramp to I-705.

In minutes you'll see polar bears. When I got out of bed this morning, I didn't expect to see polar bears.

I don't know why my neighborhood isn't considered the best in the city.

You're unable to see Commencement Bay from our house,

but you can see the houses of people who are able to see Commencement Bay.

That is a nice view.

You can go anywhere in Tacoma from East 38th.

Turn north onto East McKinley and follow it to East D Street: There's the Tacoma Dome.

Turn south onto South Steele Street: There's the Tacoma Mall.

My neighborhood may not be the best, but you can get there from here.

Mount Rainier National Park? From East 38th turn south onto Pacific and keep going.

Keep going and don't stop.

Swan Creek
Michael Haeflinger

The balloon floats over the open field
    near the mountain bike trail entrances
        on a cloudy Sunday with no rain.

The boys chase it like swallows at dusk
    plucking bugs from the river's edge.
        The balloon groups them as one unit

out beyond the felled trees towards an eastern
    din. The parents stay at the picnic tent
        drinking flavored water, beer, cold soda.

They speak of boats, ski schools, play dates, taxes.
    They gather plates of half-eaten Ritz crackers,
        half-empty juices boxes, single-munched carrots.

They watch the balloon for a moment, but
    turn their attention to the construction
        of the park, the city, their lives.

When the park was postwar-era housing
    for laborers and foremen, the roads
        must have been full of children playing

stickball or whatever they played. Tag. Hide
    and go seek. Allie allie oxen free.
        Abandoned for decades, now full of noise.

The balloon loses helium. It sinks.
    The boys cheer, descend upon it.
        One of them will carry it back perhaps

draped over his shoulder like a wild animal
    or held above his head like a title belt.
        Perhaps drug along the ground

        already on to other things.

Middle School Seminar
Rebecca Amina Echeverria

I want to tell you the story of a school
sirens in the backdrop.
City cops stare kids down as they play ball,
walk to class, eat their government lunch.

I want to tell you the story of a school
culture splashed on binders:
Islander patterns, vaquero fathers on horseback,
best friends for life, te amo, I love you.
Sarongs tied and worn in corridors,
cyphers in homeroom, beats on hollow desks.

I want to tell you a story of a school
bullets in the backdrop.
I pull my students close,
make the classroom a circle.

We read our history, start at the beginning
connect slavery to police brutality.
They weave their stories, laughing at themselves
in the middle school way, as they speak
our future into the world.

Ode to Autumn
Abbie Hughes

We begin to lose words as trees forget their leaves.
The simple gift of farewell,
of offering its life into mine.
Like the Rocky Mountain snail,
I pack my home along with me as I travel.
In so many ways,
evergreen forms the cradle of my first home.

Life happens underground in a series of brittle but fleshy roots.
Each tendril ticking a path
into the rubbled earth to rest in the darkness,
circling slightly at the tip like a fern.
The body offers itself to song,
life beginning as thunder in the throat.

I will grow and leave the shadows relishing the sunken chill
of the Puget Sound's colder depths,
Floating and diving like simple sentences by the ferry terminal.
It has turned me to air,
and can fly right through me.

Maybe it is the expanse of sky above and sea below
that soothes my soul.
Until finally the sweet whimpering of shorebirds
seduces us into sleep.
I can wade out as far as my heart can carry me.

Sentipensante of Tacoma
Bailey Lonergan

I live in the emerald temperate forest
with the tallest evergreens
and wildflowers that grow way beyond our knees.
Where the residue of rain left on the pine, keeps the air we breathe fresh.
A place where the canvas from winter to spring is gray
So, we stay in our homes and local cafe's.
A peninsula home to the Orcas, salmon, and cedar.
Where my sister and I play
in the moss and along the bay.
The stolen land of Native tribes
remembered by Mt. Rainer.
Who has watched over the town for thousands and thousands of years.
Where art is made.
Glass is blown
And the place where Chihuly calls his home.
A place with gardens that we grow
From Rosemary to Roses, and our favorite Rhododendrons
That blossom and bloom when summer approaches.
Then summer silently slips in, and our rain boots are put in the basement bins.
When the flowers bloom, and the stray cats roam
Windows and back doors swing open down every road.
My home is the Sound
Where monkeyshines are found.
My home is where the raindrops are heavy.
My home is the city of destiny.

6th is first
Jean-Pierre Garcia

You could duel pianos
Be a hippie in a house
Write in the park
Laugh in the club
Out in the park
Where lions roar
Don't cruise along ruston
Even if they're on the app anyway
The fireboat is lit
With bicycles trapped in mill bones
And haunted mansions peer over tides
The joints of the city ease and quake
Through faults all our own with arthritic grip
We grit along the division of old town union inheritance
Along the shore full of men
And those old gangsters that clawed at each other with pistols raised
The anger has simmered
To abandoned stolen kias
Slamming into the side of parked cars
Just because they can, them boys on the hill
Careless of the insurance claims and hard work an engineer has to go through
For a job that isn't even really part of the time it takes to pay it off
There was street races and cops
Do nothing be damned, do something and be twice damned
Without air
Oxygen in the blood bubbling to the Top
There's anger simmering and boiling
From the bay to the highway
We don't want this
Not the detention center,
We're not the loggers who chased chinese immigrants away
But we are along the tracks they built
Puyallup is part of that fight when they were here first and the rest of us came after.
How on earth can we reconcile the hell we gave hundreds of years ago
And not the history we are making today, years at a time
We don't rest in protest,
We work tomorrow
And paint at night

First Snow in Tacoma: A Timeline
Chloe Mohs

For a moment the air holds its breath,
gulps it down and holds on.

The gust rattles, chest burning until –

The first flake falls,
touching down.

Kissing pavement.

It's a quiet thing.
Gentle in its invasion; the steady spread.

3 AM Tacoma Time.

One minute – empty shadowed streets soaked in empty air, who sucks in a breath and
holds it till it burns.

The world turns white slowly, then,
all at once, steady in its invasion.

4 AM my dad wakes and waits for the snow to stick.

Golden light from the lamp posts beyond the window ripple into frozen pools.
Kissing pavement.

5 AM wake up call.
Whispered yelling and the hall light pooling into my sleeping eyes.
Get your layers on, it's snowing.

We'd sneak out, both of us kids.

We'd tear up the yard.
Upset the even blanket.

I'll trip over the boots I took from my mom at some point,
kissing pavement.
Dad will lift me back up steady and gentle in the hand.

When Madison Street wakes up, they'll know we were there.

Dad and I make the first tracks on Proctor.
The cold is harsh in the nose and buoyant in the heart.
Apple cider stings winter dry lips.

6 AM and Tacoma opens its eyes,
sucks in a breath (burning and rattling),
to the new world.

TACOMA THEN/TACOMA NOW
Maternal Seasons
Chelsea Eng

I. Photo Flashback: WINTER – Downtown Tacoma, 1947
Little girl, age 4, holds her mother's gloved hand
Long wool coats keep them warm
A day of shopping errands, of rifling through fabric remnants on sale
At a large table, a treasure hunting flurry
Scraps of cloth somersault in the air
She clings to her mother's coattails for fear of losing her
In a crowd of women vying for the best bits of cotton, wool, seersucker
Corduroy, silk, velvet and lace
They stop for an ice cream sundae
In the basement of The People's Store
Then to Kress' Five & Dime for buttons and ribbon
A small toy, too, she hopes! –
A little doll, a bouncing ball...
The girl is my mom, Kathie
Beside her – my grandma, Lucille

Tacoma then
    Mom was born, February 1943, at Tacoma General
    Grandma worked at an accounting firm near the Tide Flats
    "Skilled beyond her role. She could have been a CPA," Mom says.
    Grandpa Olsen worked for the Smelter
    They had a house on Shirley Street, in Ruston – dormer windows up top

Tacoma now
    A brisk December day of bright sun and clear skies
    We walk the Sea Wall
    Spot a seal making his morning rounds on the Sound
    From behind I embrace Mom's shoulders
    She clasps my hands in hers
    Her soft skin veined with life-love given over decades
    As daughter, sister, artist, wife, mother, friend; as blessing
    "I'm a Tacoma Girl," I tell her...
    "I know," she smiles.
    She is 80.

Winter then
    Christmas Eve the Olsens gathered at Uncle Harold's house on Sprague Street
    Cousins piled on the couch
    Full from a Danish dinner of Frikadeller – meatballs –
    and open-faced sandwiches – pickled herring on buttered rye
    "Mostly it was all about the dessert," Mom says,
    As Harold was a pastry chef
    Known for his Aeblekage – Danish apple cake
    At the piano – a rousing round of carols

Winter now
    Christmas Eve I head across the Narrows Bridge to Gig Harbor
    The Olsens gather at Uncle Vagn's house on Wollochet Bay
    Cousins pile on the couch
    Full from a dinner of Shirley's braised red cabbage and Louise's souffle
    I dig through Danish rice pudding topped with cherry sauce
    In search of the hidden almond that wins a prize!
    No piano, but the same carols sung cheerfully off-key

II. Photo Flashback: SPRING – North Parkway house, back deck, 1959
    Mom & Auntie Judy stand slim and tall in Easter dresses
    Squinting in the morning sunlight
    They strike cheeky poses... Oh, hats, gloves and heels!
    Before heading to church
    In the season of the Daffodil Parade on Broadway downtown

Tacoma then
    Wednesdays were their family night out
    The one night a week Grandma got a break from cooking!
    A movie at the Proctor Theater
    Then ice cream where today stands Compass Rose

Tacoma now
    I sit beside Mom at The Blue Mouse
    Polish off my "Mini Mouse Combo" before the film begins
    Cozy theater of old with emerald stained glass above
    I transport myself to a bygone Wednesday night in that same space

Spring then
    Grandma – master seamstress, maker of clothes and dolls and magic
    Canning vegetables that lined the pantry in glass jars
    Plying coffee cake and donuts from scratch
    Maiden name Zukowski
    Polish strong. One of 10 kids. 3 died of diphtheria.

Spring now
> Chipper yellow daffodils dot patches of green
> We draw deep dewy breaths
> Cute dogs and cute kids amble down Proctor
> A casual version of the parade of old, minus the elaborate floats
> Mom stands slim, if a bit less tall, these days
> In this liminal season of rain and sun, of tulips and newness

III. Photo Flashback: SUMMER – Fox Island beach at the Larsens' house, 1938
> Grandma is grinning
> Her wavy bob ends at the upturned corners of her mouth
> No wonder she liked Grandpa...
> He scoops her in his arms as if to carry her 'cross a threshold
> Though they sport bathing suits as he stands barefoot on the sand
> His football player biceps hold Grandma and her dangling legs
> Just out of high school. How young, how happy they look...
> Mom had not entered the world, nor had I – neither of us yet born
> The notion of a world without Mom in it – I can't, my breath takes leave
> I return to Grandma's radiance, settle there.

Tacoma then
> Summers were glorious! Pure delight.
> The Olsens walked to catch the Maryland boat
> Swimsuits and supplies in tow
> Bound for Vashon and a cabin on beloved Spring Beach
> Mom and her best friend, Susan, perch on the Maryland steps
> Clad in shorts, hands folded, smiles percolating
> Sunlight streaks their tousled hair
> They are intent on adventure, these two

Tacoma now
> Summer calls for a sojourn to Vashon
> A need that transcends generations... I must go!
> A cool breeze on the ferry deck, I spy jellyfish below
> Mt. Rainier knew Mom as a child, crossing these waters
> Again and again
> Back from the ferry's edge she steadies her footing in the wind
> I conjure the Tahlequah dock that was once there to greet her

Summer then
> The owners of the Maryland took Mom out on Commencement Bay
> To view the fireworks on the 4th of July
> In the season of skipping rocks at Owen Beach and Spring Beach
> Of apples turned to sauce and butter
> Of sweet corn plucked from the stalk by Grandma's sturdy hands

Summer now
> I inhale salt air mingled with ripe blackberries
> Luxurious, nourishing breath
> Having learned from the best I skip rocks at Owen Beach
> Then stroll the Rose and Dahlia Gardens in Pt. Defiance Park
> I gaze at a Summer sky so ethereal it rivals Maxfield Parrish

IV. Photo Flashback: FALL – Ruston backyard, 1949
> Mom is all of 6, hands in pockets, pocketing mischief
> Her plaid coat buttoned up 'gainst Autumn's chill
> A scarf 'round her head, tied beneath her chin
> Bare legs that will later dance professionally
> And white ankle socks tucked in Mary Janes
> She looks bemused
> By what? – I want to know

Tacoma then
> Antique Sandwich was their grocery store, source of staples and produce,
> Owned by Ray and Millie Wall
> "The only thing it didn't have was a meat market," Mom says.
> "Sometimes Dad got his meats from Blascovitch up on the hill behind the Smelter."

Tacoma now
> Antique Sandwich is my go-to for a "half-veggie on honey whole wheat"
> With chips and an appleberry juice
> In the snug glow of milk-glass schoolhouse lights
> I browse fair trade trinkets and admire the historied oak bar
> On the bench outside Mom and her best friend, Susan, chat arm in arm
> Still intent on adventure, these two
> Ruston girls, ever childhood pals

Fall then
> Meant picking huckleberries on the trail, drawing them into empty Crisco cans
> To be made into jams and muffins
> Mom could choose one new outfit from the Montgomery Ward catalog
> For the first day of school
> "We had no money for fancy, expensive clothes," she says.
> Sometimes they shopped the discount floor at Rhodes Brothers department store
> But Grandma loved to sew and made most of their clothes

Fall now
> Front porch pumpkins push color on the grey palette
> Of a cool, rainy day
> Tall trees, trees, trees form a blanket we wrap around ourselves
> Night approaches early
> I hold Mom's arm securely in mine, as I do not want her to fall
> We dodge slippery leaves on the pavement
> As we make our way to the car

Tacoma of my heart
To me you are no shadow of Seattle
You shine your own light
Across generations – in, through and beyond
Illuminated paints splash the sky above the Narrows
Love writ large of those who came before
To bestow a unique soul upon this place

I See a Valley
Elaine Briden

I see a valley,
where daffodils grow in yellow-orange rolls,
brown fields surround patches of gold,
such grandeur will take the floral parade.

I see a valley,
where my son drove the last car we owned,
newer than the rest and "more fun", he chuckled, as we
flew down the country road.

I see a valley,
where we walked under tree branches,
with light settling upon our path, when
we were a family, alone.

I see a valley,
where I practiced to be a teacher,
learning things don't come easy if you
can't conform.

I see a valley,
where Mount Tahoma reigns over all,
whose spirit burns in the hearts
of the blind but see like you, Mom.

I see a valley,
where the river is calm but mysterious,
arising from thaws of glacier snow;
once abundant with salmon but, now, depleting.

I see a valley,
where a friend is resting in a loved place, gone to
rebirth, memories of the old man
linger in my soul.

I see a valley,
where April rains make flowers bloom,
decorated on floats carrying kings and queens, like
you and me from the castle by the sea.
I see a valley.

Ode to a Gulch
Annelise Rue-Johns

A tear in the cement skin of the city
Green treetops underfoot
Looking down on a canopy
Swaying dangerously in the wind.

The world slows.
A vibrant forest
   A rushing stream
      A silent air
The squelch of footfalls
   In deep mud
A moment's respite
From the world above.

Worlds forgotten.
Remnants of what was.
A pulse - a heartbeat - a breath
Of a wild earth remembered.

Davit
Elizabeth Bradfield

>I loved the magic of the davit's block
>and tackle (rove to disadvantage), greased
>pivot that let my scrawny self hoist
>dingy from cradle, swing it out
>over water, drop down to tide. Then
>
>I could row, venture
>wherever my young arms
>could pull me along
>the rocky shore.
>   Just as easy,
>returning, hook up and haul. By myself. By
>my pre-teen self. Hard enough work
>
>to proud me. I shouldn't
>forget that. That
>would be a heavy loss.

Chapter 8

+0.01
Abby E. Murray

One day after the darkest
day of the year in the city
where I live, we gain one second
of daylight. This, I am told,
is change: a turn toward warmth
in the midst of chill even though
it is too slight for me to perceive.
And I believe in the season
of spring, that I've been there,
that I'll probably go back, just as
I believe in centuries made of months
made of seconds I can't recall.
How many injuries are healed
by the arrival of red blood cells
too small to feel as they make
their individual repairs? Light falls
on us every winter this way: one strand
at a time, each as imperceptible
as the last, countable only once
we stop to measure how much
we can see from where we are
                in the darkness.

[original poem, unpublished, written the day after the Tacoma officers who killed Manuel Ellis were acquitted, which was also winter solstice]

First Date (this is about the Browns Point Lighthouse)
Isaac Rodriguez

Across an aluminum table we exchange hearts

mine is a glaring orange, mottled with red and green.

yours is indigo, with swirls that glare back at me.

your mouth moves, silently reciting a joke

the heart speaks; it quietly asks if I will love the anger inside you

my head throws itself back, laughing noiselessly

my heart answers; will you quiet the noise in my head?

"yes", in unison

I put your heart where mine was

you do the same

we sit in the shadow of the lighthouse

Self/Portrait of Tacoma
Liz Morrow

She is
the moss burrowing down
cracks in the concrete
verdant against
stark grey
not a second glance offered
as passers by quickly
make their way to their destination.
An insistence on persisting
against all odds.

She is
in between,
and at the end,
an intersection.
Salty water lapping against
pebbled shore. Evergreen
boughs heavy with
last night's rain
and crows.

She is
ancient roots
burrowing deep in loamy
soil, blanketed in
pine needles and lichen.
The sound of her name
whispered through trees
who knew her
in youth.

And so am I.

Holy Week
Tanner Abernathy

The bogus tinsel evening, in a diabetic coma
Insulin in the electric light, bruised brownorange peaches

We pass around a terrible
secret like a long cigarette

Taxing anxiety tomorrow bursts hot polyps full of salt water and jazz
Church bells drag me across the puddle covered linoleum

The creaky window fan
hammers me with cold air

I crucify myself and then brush my teeth pull my socks
above my anxious calves

I suffer heavily in my vest of bronze & crown of pushpins
(becoming cardboard chewed by a child's square teeth)

I teach a day's worth of English class
throw myself down the stairs if anyone asked me to

Spit on the mailbox to wipe away the spider poop with the blade of my hand
I go for a walk and chew wild hemlock

I laugh and sauté wilting mushrooms
A bubbling drink simmers yellowly on the granite counter

Tarpaper ribs flatten to carpet as I write poetry
There's nothing difficult in this life

On Easter, a rainsoaked man rolls crazily down 6th Avenue
A rainsoaked man leaks lemons on Interstate 16

A shaking man is drenched in canola oil & teeters
hither and thither calling to the spirits of air

Chapels lock oakenly. Tarpcrowned graveclothes
rainsoaked on Easter sleep in gutters.

RIGHT ON, TACOMA! WRITE ON . . .
Dawn Ellis

Right on, Tacoma!
Your shining beauty and accomplishments are boundless.
Actually, what I really mean is *write on*, like
writing on the sky the words, "City of Destiny,"
like the craggy foothills of the Olympics and Cascades *write on* the horizon,
and the Narrows Bridge *writes on* backgrounds of pink sunrises and red-orange sunsets,
and like Mt. Rainier's majesty, *writes on* the Port of Tacoma.
Tacoma *writes on* to communicate all that it represents.

Imagine w*riting on* the spur of the moment,
while riding Sound Transit's Light Rail
or on a couch at Tacoma Public Library, cozy among the collection.
Imagine sitting on a bench at the Snake Lake Nature Preserve
or lounging on a blanket at Thea's Park on the Foss Waterway,
maybe even *writing on*, while watching
Grebes, Goldeneyes, and Cormorants along Ruston Way
or studying polar bears, belugas, and wolves at Pt. Defiance.
Imagine carving a heart on a tree trunk in Puget Park,
adorning it with the initials, "W.E.♡ T.Town."

There is so much more . . .
Write on your exercise log, "I climbed 30th Street again today.
Almost in shape for the killer hill on Vassault,
up to the finish line of the Sound to Narrows."
And w*rite on* the race record, Tacoma Dragon Boaters,
  "We won the final heat at the Rainier Festival!"
Write on the rental slip at Owens Beach that
you will kayak out to enjoy views of Vashon Island,
Gig Harbor, and Commencement Bay,
as sea lions laze on the rocks of the shoreline, and
harbor porpoises roll nearby, in the salt water.

Write on your athletic history, Tacoma, of
Peck Field and Cheney Stadium,
the Rainiers and OL Reign Women's Soccer.
Add your high school graduations, Tacoma Dome,
football and basketball tournaments, motorcycle races,
the Home and Garden Show, and so many other events.

"Hey, wait a minute. You forgot something.
Write on the score card that I got a Birdie on Hole 5
at Highlands Golf Course, the best little course in Tacoma."
W*rite on* a worn wooden fence, in one of the old neighborhoods,
"Love one another," and write "character," on neighborhoods of houses
where block parties and backyard barbeques were standard fare,
where children played outside until dusk, where parents said,
"Get home when the street lamps come on."
Write on Hilltop, Eastside, McKinley, and the Lincoln District,
South Tacoma, Downtown, Proctor, and the Stadium District,
Old Town, Ruston Way, and West Tacoma.
Write on the story of growing up in Tacoma, riding a bike on Five-Mile Drive,
climbing on Humpty Dumpty at Never Never Land,
and taking the bus to see an Elvis movie at the Rialto.

Write on your history, of long-standing architecture, Tacoma,
Stadium High School, the Old City Hall, McMenamins Elks Temple,
Washington Historical Society, and Union Station.
Write on your history, Tacoma, memories of
Rhodes, Peoples, Woolworth's, and Ranko's Rexall Drugs.
And *write on* the spirits of those who have passed through the doors of
Old St. Peter's, the first church built in Tacoma.

Write on the New Year, families, at First Night,
gathering with others in the Theater District to celebrate the arts.
Write on Tacoma Light Trail,
your light art illuminating the dark months
and honoring diversity, justice, and hope.
Write on perspective, Tacoma Art Museum,
bringing visitors together to experience
a wide range of American Northwest art.
(BTW, do you know about "We Rock Tacoma"
and the artists who spread messages of love and hope on rocks?
And do you *write on* a map of the city the places to search
for Monkey Shines at the Lunar New Year?)

"Hold on a sec. Can I bum a smoke?
You come to Jazz Bones often?
Ain't the music great tonight?
You like E-9 or Dirty Oscar's, too? Maybe Doyle's?
Hey, can I get your number?
Just *write on* the back of this matchbook cover."

Write on the stars that you were here, The Sonics rock band
and beloved performer Bing Crosby.
Write that you were here, Dale Chihuly, of glass blowing and Glass Museum fame,
Author Frank Herbert, Dune Peninsula's inspiration, and Cartoonist Gary Larson, of *The Far Side*.
Write on, script writers of heroes and villains, applauded by movie goers at the Grand Cinema.
And on classical music scores, Symphony Tacoma,
as your string, brass, and percussion notes reverberate throughout the Pantages.
Write on the creative spirit, Tacoma Voices, Tacoma Youth Chorus, and Tacoma City Ballet.
Write on the creative spirit, Tacoma Musical Playhouse and Tacoma Little Theater,
your performances bringing audiences to their feet in appreciation.

"Hey, isn't it a good day to hang at Wright Park?
That bench looks like a great place to sit and read.
Have you read *Dune* by Frank Herbert or *Red Paint* by Sasha LaPointe?
Here, take my copy of the *Weekly Volcano*.
Go ahead and *write on* it, to remind you of the titles. Check out the *Volcano*, too!"

Write on intellectual curiosity, Tacoma,
King's Books filling shelves with the works of wildly diverse authors.
And sit a spell with a good read, the book store cat purring on your lap.
Write on, Tacoma poets and fiction authors, playwrights, and composers.
Perform your truth during Creative Colloquy's open mic. nights
at the Living Tap Room, Shakabrah, and Alma Mater.
And *write on* the traditions of the Puyallup Elders,
the stories of the tribe whose sacred lands Tacoma rests on.
Share the Lushootseed Narratives, so the children of the tribe will learn
to walk proudly through the world, with goodness.
Write on the minds of youth, Tacoma's institutes of education,
Tacoma School District, Bates and Tacoma Community College, UPS, PLU, and UWT.
Write on, Grit City young. Let your voices be heard. Shake up the status quo.
Write on the positive changes you will make in your community.

W*rite on* justice, a checkered past that we must learn about from
The Chinese Reconciliation Park on Ruston Way.
Write on a rainbow flag, at the Tacoma Pride Festival, "We are free to love who we want to."
Write on the bricks of a Hilltop storefront a tribute to Manny Ellis, a plea for redress.
Write your initials on the wet concrete at the construction site of
affordable housing on The Hilltop, to show that you were a witness.
Write on your reader boards, Silas High School
and Hilltop Heritage, "We are celebrating a new legacy."

Tacoma General Hospital, Mary Bridge, and St. Joes, Allenmore and Wellfound,
write your healing energy on those who need care.
Tacoma Rescue Mission, *write on* the hearts of the downtrodden,
as you serve daily meals, offer shelter, and help the unhoused to work toward self-reliance.
Tacoma Community House and Tacoma Refugee Choir,
write on the collective responsibility,
helping immigrants and refugees to navigate a new culture,
and sing songs of compassion, peace, and belonging.
Write on the hearts of the hopeless, Tacoma, that there is hope.

Write on your legacy, Mayor Woodards, champion for equity and human rights,
and your legacy, Poet Laureate Christian Paige, that
you planted seeds of leadership and access for all.
Write on, Tacoma activists, leaders, and unsung heroes, that
you were vital in building Tacoma's communities.
Write on, Tacoma service organizations, like Rotary, Oasis Coffee Shop,
and the Rainbow Center, like Nourish Pierce County, Habitat for Humanity, and Aide Northwest.
Let your service records show that you encouraged others to find their best selves.

There is greatness in gathering to merge words and works together,
And you are so great at that, Tacoma.
Right on, City of Destiny, uniting old and new.
You turn darkness into light with your outstretched hand.
Write on . . .

Owen Beach: Antidote for Nonsense
Jessika Satori

Crammed in a tiny office space,
Searching for a tiny speck of grace
the lists and lists of tasks grow longer,
I want to be younger when I was stronger.

Call it the call and response, the rigamarole
dents my psyche, dings my soul
the disenchantment of life never ends
less time to myself, a tiny bit for friends.

I need the water to let me float.
Yearn for the equilibrium of a boat.
Lucy, the kayak! to water's edge,
slide 'er down from the lofty ledge.

Point both our noses to Tahlequah: North
splash wet as I go in, keep paddling forth
until the worries go and the soul remains
Opening my chapped hands to let go of the reins.

The Mountain
Riley Egge

Take a deep breath.
Whew.
Stand a moment,
Before the day steals the morning.

While walking to work
The city whizzes and buzzes
My mind in harmonious cacophony
Until I see the mountain.

When A Child Tells The Tale: Two Tacoma Neighborhoods Worlds Away
Jacqueline Ware

The Hawthorne neighborhood was all we knew.
Just across the Northern Pacific railroad tracks
by the Tacoma Sawmill

Where Hobo's knocked on doors asking for a
cup of coffee, that we gave them
because it was the right thing to do.

Where everyone had a pot of coffee brewing on the stove
for drinking and to give to Hobo's or drunk Indians
who slurred their words but would say, "sorry Ma'am."

Where we played secret agents,
tip-toeing quietly over the river and through the woods
of tall grass, pussy willows,
and into Sawmill buildings to spy for the United States,
taking back what was stolen from the Americans,
pencils, toilet tissue, and light bulbs.

Where we didn't smell anything stinky at the pulp mill, but
had fun sneaking around.
Where Spring was dreaded because large caterpillar cocoons
would be high in the trees above our heads
dropping little orange and black caterpillars all over the ground,
sometimes on us.

Where we went through a dark tunnel going to Point Defiance Park
before fancy hotels and businesses on Ruston Way were built,
and held our breaths because someone said we had to.
Where the Polar Bears were walking back and forth at the Zoo
on concrete with no snow or ice.

Where B&I had a real caged gorilla inside the store
when it should have been in the jungle with Tarzan.
Where a little red schoolhouse welcomed the children with chalkboards,
chalk for writing, and erasers for girls to clean when on punishment.
Paddles were for knuckle-headed boys
to get whacked on their palms
when they kept fooling around and acting up when the teacher said,
"Go to your seat right now and be quiet!"

Where all the neighbors knew one another and
in the summer, when school was out,
Big Momma took most of us way out to Puyallup
to pick beans or strawberries.
Where we were paid, not like the Negros we heard about
down South who used to be slaves from Africa picking cotton.

Where we went to school with white kids and Indians
and I wondered if the Indians felt sad
when we dressed up like them and
like Pilgrams for Thanksgiving
celebrations
and made Indian war cry sounds?

Where I didn't understand why the
Negro kids couldn't go to school with
white kids down South
or walk in the front door and get store credit
from Al's grocery store
when sent by mommy with a note.
Or live next to white people like our nice, old neighbors
with a cool old car in their garage,
that they let me try to crank up.
Daddy's car "old Betsy" didn't have a crank.

Where on Saturday's we could sit all day
anywhere inside the Theatre for one quarter,
after the Almond Roca factory gave us bags of
free broken candy, to watch cartoons and
movies.
Where my brother went to Hilltop to protest and
got into trouble trying to slip back in past curfew.

Where in Fourth grade things changed overnight
after a car accident and a settlement.
Our family moved just up the hill near 37th
& Mckinley Avenue where on the first day
of school at Mckinley Elementary School
the kids looked at me all bug-eyed like
they had seen a ghost.

Where I was the only Negro child, but the
teacher was nice. Where after school, a boy
called me the "n" word on the way home and
I felt like the people in the South.
Where my mom talked to the teacher and the
 principal told his parents and he stopped that
 nonsense.

Where a mixed couple moved in, but
left right away at night when their
house was toilet-papered.

Where I met Maria, the first Mexican girl I ever knew.
We played Barbie dolls, collected puzzle pieces from bubbe gum packages,
played pick up sticks, jacks, and watched Dark Shadows. Where this
neighborhood was different, where I was different, just up the hill from my
old neighborhood, but worlds away.

S. Tacoma Way (Surfaced)
Hannah Thornton

A woman yesterday, hair bleached blond and pulled atop her head,
Wearing a cheap red sundress and flip flops.

She isn't near what could be called a home.
Just industrial wasteland, littered with glass and barbed wire protected
Empty lots.

Protecting themselves from what?
The tent city down the hill, that keeps growing,
Taking city streets, forcing us to witness, smell, feel,
the long fermenting crises.
That intersecting tangle of American trauma.

Back to the woman.
Her hair is evidence that she wants to be pretty.
I think about what type of attention the simple act of donning a feminine aesthetic
Must garner around here.

Her face is a testament to that.
Twisted permanently into an almost sob.
I imagine that feeling in her chest,
Under the surface of her skin.
Twitching muscles this way and that,
Existing so long unchanged, unheard, perhaps even unsurfaced,
That the landscape of her features was forever changed.

Wright Park Conservatory
Roger Iverson

Come with me dear Nubbin sweet
to this botanical miracle
where they taffy pull green stems from bulbs
giving us spring amid our winter.

Pressed against glass walls outside is snow
piled deep and black about but in this palace grow
daffodils trumpeting spring for Daughter and Dad.
Another refuge unruffles her feathers
surprised by this bubble of spring.
I sit in slanting sun and boiler warmth
anticipating my Daughter.

Come with me my treasured heart
to soak in springtime often.
Let this be our sacred start
where roots entwine and soften.

Chapter 9

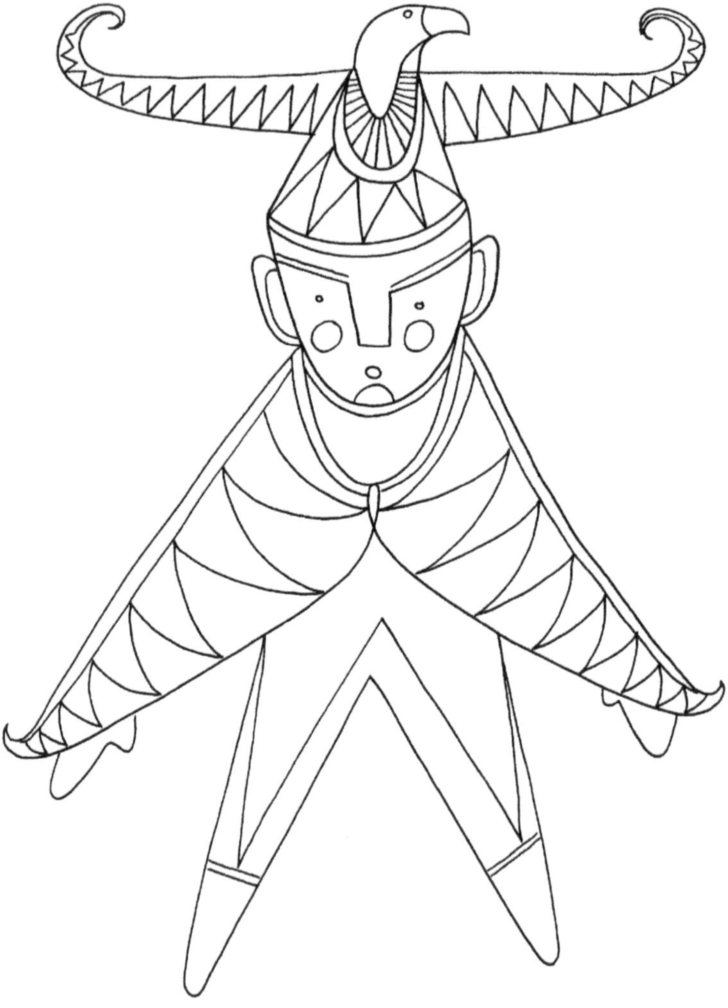

Inpatient:
Western State
Peter Jung

You dance in traffic one too many times
Chasing your anger into submission
When you get the big move
To the house where the devil discovers prospective roommates
And the writhing of your body restrained
Mirrors the worms in your memories
And sharpens the knife in your heart
You get the big move to a place
Named after a state with no name
Just a direction
And directions
And directions
To a map that someone else wrote about the worms in your brain and the ash in your soul and the wrong in your you
So you can continue traveling
In a hostage situation with no demands
West

Implication
William Kupinse

When you leave behind the ferry from Tacoma
and have been passed by the grim parade of ferried cars
gunning it up the hill, you turn left off the island highway,
pedaling steadily toward and through the vanishing point

where you are implicated, not as an exhauster of carbon,
nor as a consumer, however resistant,
nor as a member of a polity indifferent
to you and your patched and mended secondhand ways.

Instead you are the engineer and engine of a bicycle
indistinguishable from bicycles of the century past:
a lampblack parallelogram aloft two spinning circles,
rider balanced on a geometric proof.

And should someone out walking discern you featureless
in the distance, astride a palindrome of floating shapes,
you will be implicated as one small element in the momentary frame
of which road and field and trees and sky make up the greater part.

Tacoma Flora
Clover Tamayo

Living in Tacoma is like a flower growing in the asphalt cracks
You, seedling, blew away from harsher climes
You, sproutling, grow and thrive, despite being called a weed
You, brilliant and colorful, root yourself down to what existed before industrial ruin
You are not alone
    as you cleanse the Tacoma Aroma
    heal the ASARCO soil
and crack apart this concrete hell

Solo Point
Carl Papa Palmer

A mile or so down to Puget Sound
off DuPont/Steilacoom Road by Ft Lewis
the secluded military beach picnic park
open daily until dark as waves wave serene
seeing occasional coastal trains as they toot
salutes to off duty soldiers and their family.

Sharing this secret sandy shore where I brought
my lovely date to meditate in this quiet reserve
yet she'd not sit silent nor ponder just talked
texted and wandered not a single second's solace
lost her signal and complained nothing remained
except pack her and her iPhone back to Seattle.

The Buddha of Pacific Avenue
Mary Bradford

Tall.
Stately.
His was an ebony-dark face that shone with
moonlight mystery.
Donning a cape of tattered Army blanket
weathered feet soled with calloused steel
he glided along Pacific Avenue –
past the Old St. Louis Tavern
the Fun Circus
the Greyhound Station –
a Barefoot Buddha
presiding over the grit of Tacoma
back when Tacoma
was truly gritty.

Most days he floated into the old Nativity House
where a Marriott now sits
this giant, shoeless man
so intimidating to those who did not know him
and so innocent to those of us who did
always regaling us with perplexing wisdom from
his complicated brain:

Superman fell out of the sky

he told us one rainy morning,
punctuating the description with a SPLAT at the end

'cause he was thinking about Lois Lane
and you can't fly and think about Lois Lane at the same time.

Listen carefully.
You can still hear remnants of our laughter
wrapping buildings and people long-ago disappeared
in the koan of his mysterious life
this Barefoot Buddha of Pacific Avenue
spirit lingering and blessing us even now
with a reminder to pay attention
because seriously:
You really can't fly and think about
Lois Lane at the same time.

Song Of The Triple OG Bird Rescue Man
Robert Lashley

Blood is the color that mixes late September.
It tints the concrete of a late sunset mass.
It makes a mass of niggas and blackbirds.
                    The OG in white will take them.
It is on wings of those beat and broke in migrations,
those caught up in wounds and rickety structure
those lost in aroma's poisons and intoxicants
allusive until they couldn't breathe.
                    The OG in white will bring them home
Allusive is the errant gangsta disciple
as he washes his pavement of red.
Allusive is his second act with body bags
and his church with invisible chimes,
Allusive are the yellow tapes fluttering
                    In the leaves
with dust-to-dust coloring everything around it.
Lord , I'll go sweeping through the city
where my hood niggas have rolled before.

The old man claps, and cleaner particles
become a set of flying night birds.
The old man claps and ruins of a playground
become neither ruins nor a playground.
The arcs of the busted jungle gym
lift and re-sheath their pipe swords,
lift every rock that interacts with his ash
as the swing set chains stop their hanging.
                The OG in white will bring them home.
At dusk, home goings are everywhere.
Agony moves through Anglican storefronts.
Agony lies still in the gravel.
Dope boys barely make their stops now.
Dope fiends run to the water.
At dusk, the OG finds place after place
to give rosaries and proper burials.
I will stand someday by – by the river.
Won't be back on this block no damn more ...
          The OG in white will take them.
          The OG in white will bring them home

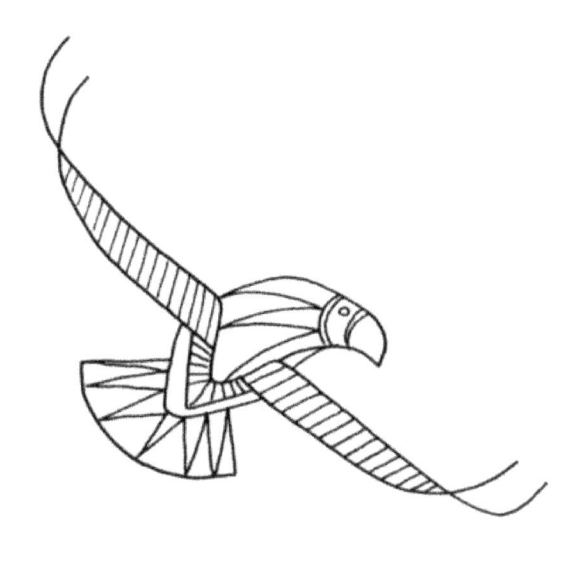

We Are Tacoma
Steve Nebel

Tacoma,
I listen to your streets roar.
It makes me feel like I belong.
I am a large truck
Rumbling down our street.
I carry the goods to the stores
Travel in the early morning light.

I am a motorcycle in a gaggle
Of fellow motorcyclists on a spring day.
I am a sports car
Muffler altered to make me sound big.

I am an unhoused man
Walking in torn clothing
Feeling the weather on my face
Hungry for a better life.
I am children walking to school
Talking excitedly on my phone
As I envision another day
With my fellow students.
I am an SUV carrying a family
On my way out of town.
There is a dog with his head out my window.
The children I am carrying
Are laughing at the happy dog.

I am taillights, headlights running along
The street reflecting my lights on
The wet pavement.
I am a new Tesla
Quietly sliding down the avenue
Slipping into a better future.
I am an old pickup truck
Driven by an enterprising poor man.
We are going around looking
For junk to find
Which we will take to the metal
Recyclers, or we will sell
Just like the drugstore down
Sixth avenue does.

I am a van with a logo
For a building contractor on it.
I am carrying the men, and materials
To a building site on Martin Luther King Avenue.

I am a container ship
Flowing into Commencement Bay
With my cargo.
I feed the trains, trucks who are
Leaving Tacoma for all places
In the continental United States.
I will leave my cargo on the Puyallup River Delta,
Depart for another port.
I will return to Tacoma someday
With another load of goods.

I am a line of cars
Relaxing down Ruston Way
On a hot Saturday afternoon,
Some of us on our way to
Point Defiance,
Some of us going to Dune Park,
Some of us wanting to be seen,
Some of us pretending to be
Invisible.
I am a resident on a busy street.
I live here.
I am Tacoma.

I am more than I could tell you here
In this writing.
Most of all - I am the people
Who live here
In Tacoma.

Ode
Nakanée Fernandez

Without fail, I greet the city as I'm coming down the hill.
"Hello, my love. You are looking... haggard."
Battered and tattered, and still it's staggering how lovely you are
to me.
I have walked these streets.
Blocked these streets.
Gritty, with a hint of something underneath;
a smile showing all its teeth
like it's got news
like it's heralding something beyond the moon &
above the sacred mountain
Beyond fractured fractals of views,
beyond clashing, gnawing blues and greys.
A message from where destiny grazes like a beast
upon that which we feed it
and maybe through haze idyllic gaze
we could see it
Through to the end of time, there's a thread
connecting to thread that
blends and blends into our foundational lense and tapestry
And actually, there's too much beauty—
too much to come after me—
to not become lyrical for this skyline is a miracle
among catastrophe.
And there's no substituting or diluting the love
for that space & time where my eyes stay glued
to that which I call mine
and I am Home.

Seeing through haze idyllic gaze
all that is yet to come:
like relentless ripples in the sound reaching for the shore
or rhododendron petals reaching for the sun.
Building
Growing
Changing
Shaping tomorrow's tomorrow;
planting seeds instead of bombs

Call me idealistic
Call it kismet
Call this love

Call this heaven
Call this hell
Call this all of the above

Be it thread, or be it ripple
Be it stone, or brick, or mud

On the skyline, tomorrow's tomorrow glistens
with our sweat, our tears, our blood

A shrine built day by day, piece by piece
Tomorrow beckons all of us.

This
Mae Murray-Angstadt

where mountains rise
like the sun
and rivers with salmon
and land rich in history
pine and maple come up
like clouds that wait
to take shape in the air
and cedars in our minds
with deer in vibrant grass groves
seagulls that fly with feathers soaring high
and seals and kelp and otters
boats that seem to fly on water
people that rise to people
and animals that rise to animals
we work together
to make this

A View of Tacoma
Aisha Lawson

Tacoma, where the aroma is indicative of nearby factories, ports and fishy waters.

A city as diverse a people as the lakes, rivers and streams.

A place where a modern home can be next to a farm or a magical garden in the middle of two high rises.

Tacoma is a place where you can experience everything or nothing and still witness the awe, from the mountains in the East to the quiet Sound in the West.

It is a city where Fall gives a mild temperament, the trees lose shade and the rain dances with fervent intensity.

Winter brings on a chill in the air, rain changes form from time to time and the city slows down to a leisurely stroll.

In the Spring, new life blooms colors of red, pink and yellow, and the leaves on trees grow into vibrant greens.

Summers are warm where gardens give way to abundant crops,

People fill the parks and vendors sell their goods amidst the backdrop of lively cultural music.

During cool rainy mornings, the mountains are dressed in fog.

During clear afternoons, the mountains are seen towering up to the sky, shrouded in layers of white.

It is a city where light breezes sway tall trees,

Waters ripple through reflections, and

Sunlight plays hide and seek with the clouds.

Eagles Every Day
Elizabeth Bradfield

    Local kids put on robes and masks we'd walked past in the museum. Materials (mountain goat hair, buttons, grizzly claws, eagle down) and context (for potlatch, to welcome back the salmon, for the dance of peace).
    Elders sang while the kids, in a range of attitude and attention found everywhere, danced. Wolf moved like the back-row guys in eighth grade math class: slumped, habituated. One boy took Raven and *was* the bird—quick stop-start tilt of eye and beak; awkward, menaced hop, a sense of bright mind turned for a while toward you, making you strange.
    He must have been thirteen. I could see the shimmer of basketball shorts, baggy and long, at the hem of his robe. And the back of his head under the mask: hair gelled to another sheen.
    This at the end of a week among the bays and islands of the Inside Passage. Drip of cedar in rain. Killer whales mid-channel. Swaths of hill bright green where the timber had been sold and taken. Gill net buoy lines. Eagles every day.

    I grew up on Tok-A-Lou Avenue, below Mana Wana and Ton-A-Wanda. Above the Puyallup's outflow. On clear days, a mountain that has not yet been returned to its name pinned the horizon.
    There was a totem pole on the lawn of my junior high that none of us ever really looked at until Todd and Wade cut it down one night with a hand saw and left it toppled in the grass.
    Everywhere, there were stylized logos with Salmon or Thunderbird, tow trucks rendered in form line design. Every year, we bought illegal fireworks from the reservation stands.
    There was head-shaking about the casinos and the fishing, talk we'd lose our house to reclamation. I drew pages and pages of black and red shapes copied from a book: ovoid, clean and full of stories I didn't bother to learn.

    We sat in the cedar room with a dirt floor and regulation fire doors. We watched and listened. The all-aboard time was 3 pm. That boy's Raven—
    We applauded then ate what they gave us: soapberries whipped to froth with sugar and handed out in paper cups stuck with carved, wooden spoons, now ours.
    The berries were sweet, then bitter.
    We filed out, saying *thank you, thank you*. Sincere. Someone, probably the purser, handed an envelope to the woman by the door. The kids milled out back in street clothes. We walked down to the boat.

Contributors

Tanner Abernathy (he/him) is a high school teacher who lives in Tacoma with his wife, rabbit, and cat. He writes poetry and tries to trick his students into writing genuinely and pursuing their interests.

Anida Yoeu Ali (she/her), Senior Artist-in-Residence, is an artist whose works span performance, poetry, installation, new media, public encounters, and political agitation. Ali has performed and exhibited at the Haus der Kunst, Palais de Tokyo, Musée d'art Contemporain Lyon, Jogja National Museum, Malay Heritage Centre, Fukuoka Asian Art Museum, The Smithsonian, and the Seattle Asian Art Museum. Ali's pioneering poetry work with the critically acclaimed performance group *I Was Born With Two Tongues* (1998-2003) is archived with the Smithsonian Asian Pacific American Program. Her works are published in *Screaming Monkeys: Critiques of Asian American Images, Voices of Resistance: Muslim Women on War, Faith and Sexuality, Shout Out: Women of Color Respond to Violence, Troubling Borders, Queering Asian American Art,* and *War, Genocide, and Justice: Cambodian American Memory Work*. Ali holds an MFA from School of the Art Institute Chicago and a BFA from University of Illinois, Urbana-Champaign.

Yuri Arakaki (they/them), most known for their work in social activism and various multimedia projects, has resided in Tacoma for the past twenty years where they have fostered an affinity towards the arts and human compassion from a young age, now expressed in their development of musical projects like BOK SUNA, involvement with the local art community, and pursuits in academia, completing undergraduate education in art, media, and culture studies, as well as pursuing a PhD in community psychology in hopes of being able to exercise the impact that compassion and creativity can have on people.

Vaquero Azul (he/they) is a transgender, two-spirit, Nahua Otomi and Taino artist. Their work focuses on trans euphoria and Mexican/Indigenous/Latine queer joy.

B. Eugene B. (he/him) is the nom de plume of Tacoma Poet Burl E. Battersby. Active in the South Sound literary community, Burl serves on the board of Write253. He has published his memoir, *B. Coming Burl* (2020), and three books of poetry, *Corrected Poems* (2020), *In A Past Life* (2022), and *Wild Rose* (2023). He is the Director of Green River College, Kent Campus. beeugenebecreative.com

Gertrude Haley Bader (she/her) was born in San Francisco in 1897. Some of her early education was received at Providence Academy, Olympia, Washington, while the academic years at Old St. Ann's Academy, Vancouver, British Columbia, was among the most valued of her life. The Nuns of the order of St. Ann de Beaupre encouraged her poetic aspirations, but, paradoxically, honors were Latin and Mathematics. Daughter of a mother well-versed in literature, Mrs. Bader learned to hear and think poetry as a small child. She met and married her husband, Francis William Bader in Tacoma in 1925 and they lived there, with their three children, until 1943. She died in July 1973, in Pasadena, Los Angeles, California, at the age of 76. Gertrude is the great aunt of Anne Bader O'Neil, who submitted this poem. This poem comes from *The Poetry of Gertrude Haley Bader*, published by Pageant Press, Inc., 1961.

Jessica J. Bloodsaw (human/she/her) currently resides in Tacoma, WA in the beautiful Pacific Northwest, remembering her roots while crawling out of her proverbial rabbit hole into the light of life. You can find her enjoying a simple existence, joyful and full of laughter, looking for connection and elevation.

Allen Braden (he/him) is the author of *A Wreath of Down and Drops of Blood* and *Elegy in the Passive Voice*. His poems have been anthologized in *The Bedford Introduction to Literature*, *Poetry: An Introduction*, *Thinking and Writing about Poetry*, *Best New Poets*, *Spreading the Word: Editors on Poetry*, *Cascadia: A Field Guide through Art, Ecology and Poetry*, *Dear Human at the Edge of Time: Poems on Climate Change in the United States*, *The Ecopoetry Anthology: Volume II* and *The World Is Charged: Poetic Engagements with Gerard Manley Hopkins*. A professor at Tacoma Community College, he lives near the historic site of Fort Steilacoom in Lakewood, Washington.

Elizabeth Bradfield (she/her) grew up in Browns Point and graduated from Stadium High School. Now a poet/naturalist living on Cape Cod, her seven books include *Interpretive Work*, which won the Audre Lorde Prize in Lesbian Poetry, *Toward Antarctica*, and *Cascadia Field Guide: Art, Ecology, Poetry*, winner of a 2024 Pacific Northwest Book Award. Editor-in-chief of *Broadsided*, Liz teaches at Brandeis University and works as a naturalist and field assistant. *www.ebradfield.com*

Mary Bradford (she/her) is a retired hospice social worker who occasionally wrangles middle-schoolers as a sub in Tacoma Public Schools. She got rid of her car a few years ago and never looked back. Mary can be found wandering through Tacoma on foot, bicycle, or on Pierce Transit. She blogs at *www.gringavieja.blogspot.com*.

Elaine Briden (she/her) was born on Blackfeet Indian reservation in Browning, MT and is an enrolled member of the Blackfeet tribe. She lived on the reservation until she was 10 years old then moved to Washington state. Her family lived in Yakima and Seattle before settling in Tacoma in 1967. She has five brothers and five sisters, one son, and graduated from Stadium high school in 1970.

Andrea Clausen (she/her) is an Iowa native who recently celebrated her twenty-year anniversary in Washington State and calls Tacoma her adopted hometown. Andrea holds a J.D., an M.F.A in creative nonfiction, and an M.A. in English. When she is not writing, you can find her exploring Tacoma on her bike, checking out the Grand Cinema's newest independent films, and enjoying Washington's abundant local breweries with her partner Nate.

Sam Cori (she/her) is a Tacoma singer/songwriter, instrumentalist, Voice Actor, and Audiobook Narrator. She has a background in musical theater, classical voice and has been playing piano since age 7. She has narrated 11 full-length audiobooks and has trained in voiceover with Aliki Theofilopoulous, Bob Bergen, Marc Graue, Melissa Hutchison, and Sally Clawson. She is in love with Bob's Java Jive and can be found there regularly performing karaoke and becoming Alice in her Alice in Wonderland themed shows. Sam writes quirky, romantic, sexy music for the people of Tacoma; fan favorites include Tacoma anthems, *"Douche Bag"*, *"Dad Bod"*, *"Douche Bag 2"*, *"Oh, Lucy"*, *"Miss Frizzle"*, and *"Mama Needs Her Wine and Chips"*. She has played recently at The Valley, Bob's Java Jive, Mad Hat Tea Co., Heritage Coffee House, Water from Wine, Darrell's Tavern, The Charleston, Nate Jackson's Super Funny Comedy Club, and Porchfest. She recently opened for T.I. and the Haha Mafia at SFCC. She loves The Beatles and Gertrude Stein.

Karen Cruz (she/her) was born in Longmont, Colorado, and began writing at an early age. She is the author of the poetry collection *The Yearlong Suicide*, published in 2019. When she is not writing poetry or prose, she competes in weightlifting and runs a small business out of Tacoma, Washington, where she currently resides.

Frank D'Andrea (he/him) is a resident of Tacoma. He is a former writing instructor and recovering poet.

Albert 'Al' de Santis (he/him) is a local architect and has published a few poems, a fact he sprinkles in conversations like a Harvard grad does 'Haaavaaad.' When he's not working he's doing things other people would consider work but that he actually enjoys. He loves very few people and can't say who because the wrong ones always think it's them and they are the ones with the … in her aunts. wink wink. Al went to College, but not as good as… He cut two umbilical cords that act more mature than he is. He climbed topless mountains literally and figuratively and he enjoys literature and figures excluding numbers. He has not seen ghosts, aliens, or the northern lights but has smelled urine inside the Great Giza Pyramid and witnessed many other wonders both natural and man-made and strives to be as mysterious and delicious as soup dumplings.

Melody Derrick (she/her), AKA "Felix Rex" has performed poetry both live and on college radio in Las Vegas. She has lived in the Pacific Northwest since 1998 and on the Peninsula since 2008. She tries to create poems that connect the reader with the natural world and the passage of time on a human scale. Winner of the Hiram Hunt Poetry Award at her alma mater, UNLV.

Rebecca Amina Echeverria (she/her) is a Queer Muslim Poet and Teacher living in Tacoma, WA. She is interested in working with community to make the world a more livable place. She enjoys cooking, reading, and hiking with her two children.

N.L. Edwin (she/her) is an American author, artist, musician, and comedian, but you'll just have to take her word for it. She has a master's degree in Cognitive Neuroscience from Freie Universität in Berlin, Germany which has proven to be, to her dismay, utterly useless. She jogs once a week at Point Defiance for her mental health, not to lose weight. She writes poems and bi-lingual children's books (English/German) when she's not busy searching for and applying to jobs she can't get because the gap in her resume is just too large to be trusted. Being true to herself and helping others is of utmost importance to her.

Xandra Egge (she/her) is a poet and visual artist who grew up in East Tacoma, frequenting the Moore Branch library for audiobooks and the Cost Less on Pac Ave for Dum Dums.

Riley Egge (he/him), a Tacoma born native, musician and poet, grew up immersing himself in music and creative expression. Influenced heavily by the beauty of the outdoors, Riley discovered a passion for weaving words and penning poems. Riley enjoys capturing universal feelings onto the page, from love to heartbreak to existential soul cries.

Dawn Ellis (she/her) retired three and a half years ago from a 37-year career in secondary education, as an English and History teacher. Since retirement, she has been an avid golfer and a member of the McCormick Woods and Highlands Golf Courses. She earned a spot at Gamble Sands two summers ago with her partner, in the Washington Golf Net Four Ball Match Play Tournament. Dawn's other loves are pickleball and hiking. When she retired, Dawn formed a women's hiking group, called the Sole Sistas. Hiking and growing up on the beach in Gig Harbor are Dawn's primary influences on her other love, writing. Dawn is active in Creative Colloquy, submitting pieces to the on-line and print publications, as well as being a featured reader and reading during Open Mic. at CC's monthly gatherings.

Chelsea Eng (she/her) is a dancer and writer who loves and has deep roots in Tacoma, though she is based in San Francisco. She has spent extended periods of time in Tacoma each year since her mother, a Tacoma Ruston native, was pregnant with her. Chelsea's short film work has screened in the 2020 and 2022 Destiny City Film Festivals; her related quote made the *Tacoma News Tribune*. As an Argentine Tango professional with over 25 years of experience, Chelsea did a 2023 guest residency – teaching and performing – at the University of Puget Sound. Since 2020 Chelsea has written soul-baring personal narrative for the purpose of tikkun olam, the Jewish concept of healing the world. After completing the 2024 Vashon Artist Residency as a writer, Chelsea became an Abby Freeman Artist in Residence (writer) with Los Angeles-based theater company The Braid/Inspiring Jewish Stories. Returning to wondrous Tacoma recharges Chelsea's spirit.

Nakanée Monique Fernandez (she/they) is a multidisciplinary artist and activist from Tacoma, WA who takes her inspiration from all the great and terrible beauties of this world. Born from music(love) and anointed by word & colour, you can find them in the forest or the water... or on Instagram.

Internationally published author **Claudia Riiff Finseth** (she/her) loves to explore what it means to live and grow as a human being. A native of Washington State, Finseth holds a BA in English and a BSN in Nursing from Pacific Lutheran University. She was mentored by the late Washington state poets Sam Hamill and R.P. Jones, and has won poetry awards. The late Tacoma composer Sara Glick used several of Finseth's poems for lyrics for her choral works. Her poem, "Invoking Auden and the Goddess", appeared in *Mute Note Earthward*, the 2006 anthology of the Washington Poets Association. She lives on one of the many lovely creeks that run through Pierce County and out into the Salish Sea.

Jean-Pierre Garcia (he/him) is a stream of conscious, slam inspired poet based in Tacoma, WA. Originally from Southern California, he writes from a latinx and LGBTQ+ perspective. Working in public media, education and events industries; he loves sad jams, bargain bin diving for his record collection, a growing book/shelf ratio and good tea. He lives with a gamer paraeducator and wildly propagating succulents. - "It's a good life."

In matters of poetry, **David Gilmour** (he/him) has been writing verse since he was a teenager, a lover of antique Robert Burns and the new-fangled Theodore Roethke. Lately his Seattle friend, Koon Woon of Goldfish Press has introduced him to serious and frivolous Chinese poetry. In his years in Tacoma he belonged to poetry circles, a long standing member of Connie Wallie's Poetry Connection, till life got too busy. For Poetry Connection in the 90s, he played poetry emcee at Prosito's Restaurant on 6 th Ave, and for two years at Café WA (now Bluebeard's spot). Still have a folder of works and the sign-up sheets. Since Viet Nam days, he marched against America's insane 21st-century wars, made street art to irritate viewers, attended salons and delivered talks on antiwar posters. Now at KTAH Radio (http://radiotacoma.org/sound-poetry/) he hosts "Sound Poetry" interviews.

Kristy Gledhill (she/her) - A Michigan native with a soft spot for the place that raised her, Kristy Gledhill has called the Pacific Northwest home for the past 30 years. A yoga teacher and antiracist activist, she writes from the unceded Coast Salish land colonially known as Gig Harbor, Washington. She earned an MFA from The Rainier Writing Workshop at Pacific Lutheran University in 2021 and her work has appeared in *Terrain.org*, *Dunes Review*, *Creative Colloquy*, *Sonic Boom Press*, *Beyond Words* and *Sweet Lit*. Her poems have also appeared in the gardens at Lakewold Gardens and at the Pacific Bonsai Museum.

Maizy Apple Green (she/her) is 20 years old and was born and raised in the North End of Tacoma, Washington. She is a proud graduate of Old-Town Co-Op, Washington Elementary School, Mason Middle School and Stadium High School. She is currently attending the University of Washington in Seattle where she is majoring in English Language and Literature and double- minoring in Classical Studies and Art History. She is also President of the UW Poetry Club and a copyeditor at the UW Daily. She is also a big fan of Taylor Swift, doing yoga, playing golf, reading, dancing by herself (or with her friends), and writing poems.

Michael Haeflinger (he/him) is a poet from the Midwest who resides in Tacoma, WA.

Erik Hanberg (he/him) has published more than ten books, including *Semi/Human* and *The Lattice Trilogy* and four books for nonprofit leaders. His books have sold more than 100,000 copies and have been translated into Spanish, Italian, Portuguese, and Arabic (long story). He has lived in Tacoma all his life and has served on the MetroParks of Tacoma, in marketing at KNKX Public Radio, and as the Managing Director of the Grand Cinema. You might have also heard his voice on several Channel 253 podcasts, which he co-founded in 2017.

Susan Harmon (she/her) was a former radio host for the Susan Harmon Experience, SHE, on 1150 am KKNW. She focused on spirituality and social justice. Susan's desire is to be an agent for change and to open communication between people who think they have nothing in common with each other. In that process, she examined her own prejudices while actively listening to others. Creating Peace within her own sphere of influence is a beginning.

Phil Harty (he/him) is an educator, musician, aspiring poet and longtime resident of Tacoma, Washington who highly values the connections between creativity and community. Phil Harty has played in multiple music projects in Tacoma, has recently produced his first poetry podcast, and is currently in graduate school at Evergreen State College to become an English Language Arts teacher. He is inspired by the reciprocal interactions in nature and views writing as a way to listen deeply, reflect and understand connections between the relationships between living beings and land.

Sarah Heavin (she/her) is a licensed psychologist and professional expert witness, testifying on the developmental impact of traumatic life events. She used to write a lot of poems on the floor of her bedroom with a Janet Jackson CD in the background. Then, she grew up and poems seemed like something only teenagers did, so she stopped writing. Luckily, the universe reminded her who she really is and she is back again, only now she has a muse and listens to Run the Jewels. Sarah isn't just a psychologist. She is a good mom, a good friend, and a lover of Tacoma. She hopes you like the poem enough to ask her to write another.

Micah Ackerman Hirsch (they/them) is an author, chess coach, and environmental educator. Although they no longer live in Tacoma, a piece of it lives in all that they love and all that they create.

Alexa Brockamp Hoggatt (she/her) is a Pacific Northwest based writer interested in the changing meaning of "home", and its relationship to family, ancestry, and choice. Her work has previously been published in *Beyond Words Magazine*, *Sky Island Journal*, *Strait Up Magazine*, and *Free Verse Revolution*.

Abbie Hughes (she/her) is a writer and undergraduate student in the BA English program at Pacific Lutheran University. Her work has been published in *Saxifrage Literary Journal* Volumes 48, 49, and 50. She lives in University Place, Washington where she continues to enhance her craft and eventually hopes to further pursue her studies through an MFA creative writing program.

Find out more about **Roger Iverson** (he/him) at *www.RogerIverson.com*.

render jemis (they/them) is an artist, poet, and zinester residing on the ancestral homelands of the Puyallup people. Like their art, they live at the intersection of Black experience, queer longing, chronic divergence, and cosmic awe. They like to spend their free time playing Hearthstone and drawing copious amounts of lines.

Peter Jung (he/him) is an autistic queer disability advocate from Hilltop. He has 8 years of experience working in crisis and intensive mental health services, and utilizes art and games like Dungeons and Dragons to help autistic teens and adults build community and self advocacy skills.

Sandy King (she/her/they/them) moved from Central Wisconsin to Tacoma in 1989. She enjoys writing poetry, short stories, and an occasional essay. She also makes oil pastel and ink drawings, sings in a choir, swims, and attends the occasional drop-in ballet class. She has been published in local projects such as *Wrist Magazine*, the *Tacoma Laureate Listening Project*, *Inquietudes Literary Journal*, *The Moss Piglet*, and a handful of *Creative Colloquy Literary Anthology* volumes, and has had the honor of being a featured reader for Tacoma City Ballet's Mid-Winter Masquerade Ball Soiree, the Creative Colloquy Lit Crawl, and the Vision 2025 Literary Festival.

John Kulm (he/him) lives, part time, on a family farm, close enough to The Gorge Amphitheater to hear the bass, but far enough away to avoid the traffic. He has a home in Tacoma, walking distance from his favorite bar for Taco Thursdays. John has read his work at The National Cowboy Poetry Gathering, The National Poetry Slam, and countless tours of one-nighters.

William Kupinse (he/him) is Professor of English at the University of Puget Sound, where he teaches British literature, creative writing, and environmental humanities. He was Tacoma Poet Laureate from 2008-2009.

Robert Lashley (he/him) was a 2016 Jack Straw Fellow, Artist Trust Fellow, and a nominee for a Stranger Genius Award. His books include *Green River Valley* (Blue Cactus Press, 2021), *Up South* (Small Doggies Press, 2017), and *The Homeboy Songs* (Small Doggies Press, 2014). His poetry has appeared in *The Seattle Review of Books*, *NAILED*, *Poetry Northwest*, *McSweeney's*, and *The Cascadia Review*, among others. In 2019, *Entropy* named The Homeboy Songs one of the 25 essential books to come out of Seattle. *I Never Dreamed You'd Leave In Summer* is his first novel.

John Lawrence "The Undertaker" (he/him) is a lifelong Tacoma resident. A father of three. He has enjoyed writing and storytelling since the moment he was able to do so. A licensed funeral director, he has cared for the dead and their families in Tacoma for well over a decade. In his free time he is a professional fighter and coach and enjoys playing video games with his sons.

Aisha Lawson (she/her) is an artist of over two decades and has always loved poetry. Her art represents fine art, photography and occasionally she likes to write poetry to express feelings on paper. She has participated in several community art sales selling arts and crafts, exhibitions, and local festivals around Tacoma like MOSAIC. Aisha has also donated art for charity at art auctions and volunteered at TAM. Aisha is originally from Federal Way but has called Tacoma her home for several years.

Bailey Lonergan (she/her/hers) has spent most of her life living in Tacoma, Washington. She attended first through twelfth grade in Tacoma Public Schools and loved growing up in the north end/6th Ave area. After graduating from Silas High School she moved to San Diego where she attend San Diego State University. Since spending time away from Tacoma she found herself missing it more and more. She always loved the art and uniqueness of the city, and the beautiful sense of community it offers. Some of her favorite things to do when visiting home on break are going thrifting at Scorpio Rising, driving around 5 mile drive in Point Defiance, or grabbing some delicious food at the farmers market.

Beverly Mathews (she/her) has lived in the Puget Sound area all her life. All 73 years of it. She enjoys Tacoma, the mountains, water and weather.

Emily Meyer (she/her) has written poetry since she was a teenager attending Tacoma School of the Arts. Now, as an adult facing the prospect of leaving Tacoma, she is naturally reflecting on the twenty years she has lived in this city. In that time she has gained three cats and a bachelor's degree in creative writing at the University of Puget Sound.

Kevin Miller (he/him) - MoonPath Press published Miller's collection of baseball poems, *Spring Meditation*, in 2022. His collection *Vanish* received the Wandering Aengus Publication Award in 2019. Pleasure Boat Studio published *Home & Away: The Old Town Poems* in 2009. Blue Begonia Press published *Everywhere Was Far* in 1998. *Light That Whispers Morning*, from Blue Begonia Press, won the 1994 Bumbershoot/Weyerhaeuser Publication Award. Miller lives in Tacoma.

Chloe Mohs (she/they) is a queer writer born and raised in Tacoma, Washington. They graduated from Tacoma Community College in 2023 and are now working part time while working on different writing projects. Mohs keeps plants for company and splits custody of her cat with her parents. Currently they are trying to write their first novella in hopes of being published.

Liz Morrow (she/her) is a multidisciplinary artist and writer hailing originally from Anchorage Alaska. She now resides in Tacoma on the unceded homelands of the Puyallup and Coast Salish peoples. Her art, both visual and written, focuses on elevating the mundane, and pulling apart the threads of normal everyday life and objects through the lens of poetry and art. Her work also wrestles with the push and pull of indigenous and colonizer identities as a woman of mixed ancestry, both European and Unangax̂, in the diaspora.

Jack Morrow (he/him) is a seven year old boy living in Tacoma. He likes to play games, make books, and snuggle with his mom. When he grows up, he wants to be a scientist and discover something no one has ever discovered before. His favorite thing about Tacoma is the nature around it.

Gloria Joy Kazuko Muhammad [Joy] (she/her) is a literary arts teaching artist, writer, filmmaker, editor, and community organizer based in Puyallup Territory (Tacoma, WA). As a writer, Joy is inspired by spirituality, everyday life, nature, music, and cinematography. She is a graduate of Washington State Teaching Artist Training Lab and facilitates writing workshops rooted in healing and personal development. Additionally, she facilitates professional development workshops with teachers on utilizing social-emotional learning, is a consultant for curriculum development for youth and adults arts programming, and is always down to be a speaker on collective care! An ongoing learner, Joy cares about building community, environmental justice, and co-creating a world in which we're all free.

Roxann Murray (she/her) is an award-winning neurodivergent photographer based in Tacoma. Roxann is a known biophiliac; since she was a child, she has had a strong connection with the natural world. Growing up in the Pacific Northwest, Roxann developed an affection for trees, fungi, ferns, and the seashore. Since she is Nakota and Dakota on her father's side, she tries to view the world through a decolonized perspective and live in a way that she hopes make her ancestors proud. When she's not shooting and editing photographs, Roxann is reading, exploring, gardening, or planning her next adventure.

Abby E. Murray (she/they) is the editor of Collateral, a literary journal concerned with the impact of violent conflict and military service beyond the combat zone. Her book, *Hail and Farewell*, won the Perugia Press Poetry Prize and was a finalist for the Washington State Book Award. She served as the 2019-2021 Poet Laureate for the city of Tacoma, Washington, and currently teaches rhetoric in military strategy to Army War College fellows at the University of Washington.

Mae Murray-Angstadt (she/her) is a fourth grader at Grant elementary. This is her first published poem, but she writes often and has gotten some of the best grades in writing in her class. She does after school basketball and is trying out for point guard. Her favorite books are the Wings of Fire series and selections from her mother's poetry library.

Steve Nebel (he/him) is a self-published poet with one book, *Remembering the Twenty-First Century*. He has lived in Tacoma with his wife Kristi since 1997. They play music together with their friend, Gen Obata under the name "Cosmo's Dream", and as a duo as "Steve and Kristi Nebel". Steve is also the editor for the local radio show, "Sound Poetry" which he produces with his friend, David Gilmour. The show airs on KTAH, Radio Tacoma at 8am, and 8pm each day.

Tom Nolan (he/him) was born and raised in Tacoma. He graduated from the University of Portland. Tom studied abroad in Salsburg, Austria. He has worked and performed on television. Tom wrote a novel *Zero In*.

francis faye oak (she/her) is a queer trans woman attempting to soften her approach toward life, be precise with her words, and honest about her limitations. her work bears witness to the way grief teaches her how to stay alive & live as an expression of trans joy. she rents an apartment in tacoma, wa & lives alongside two cats, a child, and many other miracles.

Joshua Olver (he/him) is an actor, writer, and all around chill dude who has lived in Tacoma with his wife Mo and daughter [Name redacted] since 2020.

Carl "Papa" Palmer (he/him) of Old Mill Road in Ridgeway, Virginia, lives in University Place, Washington. He is retired from the military and Federal Aviation Administration (FAA), enjoying life as "Papa" to his grand descendants and being a Franciscan Hospice volunteer.

Tia Pliskow (she/her) has spent her entire life in the beautiful South Puget Sound region. After graduating from the University of Puget Sound with a BA in Creative Writing, she became a teacher and earned a Doctorate in Education. She chose to remain in the area to raise her family and can't imagine living anyplace else. Dr. Pliskow continues to give back to her community as a professor currently in her twelfth year at Tacoma Community College. Her work has appeared previously in such publications as *Simply Haiku* and *SchoolArts Magazine*

Tammy Robacker (she/her) graduated from the Rainier Writing Workshop MFA program in Creative Writing, Poetry at Pacific Lutheran University (2016). She won the 2015 Keystone Chapbook Prize for her manuscript, *'R'*. Her second poetry book, *Villain Songs*, was published with MoonPath Press (2018). Tammy served as Poet Laureate of Tacoma during 2009-2010 and is a Hedgebrook writer-in-residence. She published her first collection of poetry, *The Vicissitudes*, in 2009 (Pearle Publications) with a generous TAIP grant award. Tammy's poetry has appeared in *Harpur Palate*, *FRiGG*, *concis*, *Tinderbox*, *Alyss*, *Menacing Hedge*, *Chiron Review*, *Duende*, *So to Speak*, *Crab Creek Review*, *WomenArts*, and many more. Tammy was born in Germany, raised in Pennsylvania, lives in Washington, and works in education technology.

Isaac Rodriguez-Corona (he/him) is a burgeoning poet hailing from the hills of Tacoma, Washington. He's a senior in college. When he's not learning, Isaac can usually be found exploring new culinary delights in his city, or staying in and watching Frasier. No in-between.

Annelise Rue-Johns (they/any) is a naturalist, ecologist, and poet in Tacoma. Their work is often inspired by the intersection of human and wild spaces.

Jessika Satori (she/her) lives and works in Tacoma. She is a poet, writer, professor, entrepreneur, educator and artist. She has written three poetry chapbooks: *I'm a Product of Thomas Jefferson's Seventh Generation*; *The Angle of Repose: Poems about Geology*; and *Come to My Dinner Party*. She will release a fourth chapbook this year, *ROY G BIV, Poems Regarding Science*. She has a coaching and consulting company, A Creative Force, which trains and develops leaders to use their creative abilities. Jessika is a professor, teaching not only in the US, but in UAE, South Korea, Russia and Madagascar. She has studied poetry with Anne Waldman, screenwriting with Stewart Stern and songwriting with Sharon Vaughn and Shelly Poole.

Celeste Schueler (she/her) is originally from Mississippi but now resides in the Pacific Northwest. She has her BA in English and MFA in creative writing from Mississippi University for Women and has taught poetry workshops at the Tacoma Public Library. Celeste loves taking her twin daughters on various adventures in and around Tacoma as well as reading all sorts of books and writing poetry.

Jacque Lynn Schultz (she/her) is an award-winning writer, lecturer and performer who has called downtown Tacoma home for the last 10 years. She moved to Tacoma after dedicating 30 years of her working life to a national animal welfare organization located in New York City through which she worked with humane organizations in 49 of the 50 states and the District of Columbia.

John Sexton (he/him) is, which is a source of great trouble. He is, most of the time, in Tacoma, Washington.

Lucas Smiraldo (he/him) is a poet, playwright, equity and justice professional and collaborative artist who often creates performances fusing spoken word with music, drama, dance and other creative genre. In 2014-2015 Lucas was the Poet Laureate for the City Of Tacoma and launched an oral history program called the "*Laureate Listening Project*" featuring the audio work of 50 grassroots poets exploring the spirit of place in Tacoma which is now available at the Tacoma library website: *https://northwestroom.tacomalibrary.org/index.php/laureate-listening-project-recordings*. Lucas's latest project was the creation of his book *365 Revolutions*, *https://www.365revolutions.com* a fully illustrated set of poems to represent every day of the year inspired by yoga poses and liberation poetry. He is currently working on a new play titled "Savor" , which explores end of life stories informed by food, family and sacred passings.

Meredith Smith (she/her) is a former resident of Tacoma's hilltop neighborhood. Though she now lives in Ballard, she still writes poetry, fiction and music among the emerging townhomes. Her poem in this anthology was written in Tacoma in the early 2000s. Her more recent work has appeared in *The Cryptonaturalist*, *The Gravity of the Thing*, and elsewhere. An alumna of the Hugo House, she does not have a degree in creative writing.

Jessica Stovall (she/her) knew she wanted to live in Tacoma from the first time she visited during her Junior year of high school. She graduated from Pacific Lutheran University with a degree in Elementary Education, and she taught 1st grade and Kindergarten for 14 years before pivoting to the world of non-profit social services. Jessica now works as the program coordinator for Santa for Seniors, and she loves finding new ways to help seniors feel recognized and connected to the community. She and her 6-year-old daughter love to visit the Tacoma Public Library, and she can't wait for the renovations at the Main Branch to be completed! When the weather allows, she also loves to walk to Gateway to India with her partner to enjoy the malai kofta and paneer pakoras. She has enjoyed reading poetry for years, but she's only recently decided to try her hand at writing.

Clover Tamayo (they/siya) is a nerdy neurodivergent enby Pilipinx abuse survivor who enjoys connecting with folx through stories. Siya founded Clover Daydreams: a safe and inclusive book space, which centers stories for and by BIPOC, Queer, Trans, Disabled, and Marginalized folx. The Clover Daydreams Book Space is tucked away in Black Sheep Resale, a curated vintage clothing store and queer oasis. Both are located on the unceded territory of the Puyallup People in South Tacoma.

Hannah Thornton (she/her) moved to the Hilltop neighborhood in 1996 as a military brat. She fell in love with the duck ponds of Wright Park, the brick covered hills, and couldn't believe her luck at having a view of the sea from her elementary school playground. She began writing books as soon as she was able, eventually terrorizing Tacoma with her dramatic poetry and short stories a SOTA student. Now, Hannah is a mother to two beautiful boys and happily serves the community as a special education teacher for the Tacoma School District. Hannah continues to make art through writing as her favorite pastime.

Felicia Tran (she/her), a second-generation Chinese (Teo Chew) and Vietnamese American woman, lives in Tacoma, Washington on the traditional lands of the Puyallup Tribe of Indians. She is a Master of Arts in Theology & Culture graduate of The Seattle School of Theology & Psychology and intends to facilitate learning spaces that engage liberative theologies. Her current research interests are in land rights and narrative ethics that intersect with migration and indigeneity in the Pacific Northwest and Asian American feminist theology. Felicia worked with college students in the Puget Sound area for nine years and currently works for The Allender Center. She loves chatting and imagining hypotheticals, but as a deep introvert, she is often found recovering from socializing with people she loves. She finds cozy slippers, a good sci-fi show, tea, and Chinese herbal soups a perfect remedy combination for her social hangovers. Her favorite poet is Li- Young Lee.

Josie Emmons Turner (she/her) lives on an estuary feeding into Gig Harbor. She is a retired teacher and is an avid gardener, amateur French cook. Turner served as Tacoma Poet Laureate 2011-2013. She has been published in numerous anthologies and her poems have been set to music in song cycles for secular and liturgical settings.

Julie Van (she/her/hers) is a Vietnamese-American educator and writer who believes that stories have the power to inform, educate, inspire, and connect. She is passionate about sharing her love for exploring the unknown, igniting curiosity, and empowering others to share their unique perspectives. She earned a B.A. in Mathematics at the University of Washington and M.Ed from the University of Massachusetts Amherst in Higher Education Administration. She loves anything that gets her out of her head and into her body, and she will try anything new at least once. She loves snowboarding, backpacking, hiking, climbing, yoga, writing/poetry, and exploring new places through food. A Pacific Northwest native, Julie currently resides in Tacoma, Washington.

Katherine Van Eddy Dizon (she/her) is a California-born poet who now lives in Washington State. Her poems have appeared in journals such as *Common Ground Review*, *Creative Colloquy*, *Gold Man Review*, *Cirque*, and *Clover*. She has a BA in Creative Writing, MAT in Elementary Education, and MFA in Poetry from Pacific Lutheran University. Katherine loves mothering her kids and her cat, Dexter. She feels most at home anywhere near water.

Christina Vega (they/them) is a Queer Chicana poet from the borderlands of Texas & New Mexico. Their mother is Anita Vega,and their grandmother is Aurora Vega. They live on Puyallup and Nisqually Land. They're also a single parent. Christina is the publisher at Blue Cactus Press, where they make books that serve as tools for self-empowerment, personal transformation, and liberation; for and by folks from historically marginalized groups. Christina published their first full-length poetry collection, *Maps*, in 2017, a chapbook co-published with Conner Bouchard-Roberts of Winter Texts called *Decay* in 2022, and their sophomore poetry collection, *Vega*, in 2023. Christina believes we have the power to reshape our communities with principles of Emergent Strategy, transformative justice, and collective laboring of love. They believe revolution starts at home.

Jacqueline (Jaye) Ware (she/her) was born and raised in the Pacific Northwest. Her meat and potatoes are in the legal profession, but she butters her bread as a poet, spoken word artist, and recent playwright. Jaye is drawn to performance material that creatively captures unique children's stories, and social justice and injustice issues. With a special fondness for children and seniors, she frequently writes stories and prose geared towards their age range and interests. She is a member artist with the 4Culture Touring Arts Roster and the African American Writers' Alliance. Her short "on location" staged play titled; *Madison Park Bench* is located at: *https://www.youtube.com/watch?v=f4CxxMRO8nw&feature=share* Her short pandemic musical titled, *COVID Dreams* is available at *https://vimeo.com/ondemand/pandemicplayscoviddreams*. Jaye is the founder of the group, Four Black Women Talking. These professional, seasoned with salt women, were born/raised in four different regions of the Country during civil rights and Jim Crow. They share their personal experiences, upbringing, education, and how it shaped and molded who they are today as artists. She has performed spoken word at Madaraka festival, Town Hall, local libraries, senior centers, major museums, on Orcas and Vashon Island, schools, bookstores, art galleries, and many other venues. Published: *Anthologies: Voices That Matter* and *Black Writers Unmasked*, by African American Writers' Alliance Anthology: *Good Word Walking, A Western WA Poets Network Anthology*, by East Point West Press. Black Minds Publishing (online), Poem titled, "A Black Poem." Social Media:@4BlackWomenTalking @WareoftheWords

Born in Tacoma and raised in Southwest Washington, **Trevor Neil White** (he/him) lives and works in Grit City as an attorney by day and a poet/fantasy-horror storyteller by night. He is a graduate of the University of Washington, with a B.A. in English and Creative Writing, and Cornell Law. His work has been published in the UW journals *AU* and *Bricolage*, Phi Theta Kappa Honor Society's *Nota Bene*, and *Sanitarium Magazine*. He has also self-published two collections of short fiction and poetry, with a third on the way. In his spare time, he enjoys video games, producing YouTube videos, and defending emo music. His creative blog is at *https://notesandsketches.blog*, and you can follow him on Instagram at @TNW24.

Delvis George (they/them) attends IDEA High School and is interning with Voices of Tacoma. In addition to working on marketing and the editorial review process, Delvis helps run the community events and also finds time to write poetry.

Mauricio Robalino (he/him) creates colorful and whimsical artworks using a variety of materials, especially mosaics. His artworks are inspired by multicultural artistic traditions. In his own words, "My art is a celebration of life, nature, and hope." Robalino was born and grew up in Ecuador. He earned a Bachelor of Fine Arts degree from the San Francisco Art Institute in 1983 and a Master of Fine Arts degree from the University of California at Santa Barbara in 1988. He is based in Tacoma, Western Washington.

Omar Willey (he/him) is a polymath polyglot polymorphously perverse poet person publishing photography and prose at The Seattle Star.

Credits

Abby E. Murray, "Tahoma Doesn't Love Us" (2), from *Grit City Magazine*, Hard Copy 10, December 2020. Reprinted with permission.

Elizabeth Bradfield, "At the Source of the Ore our Smelter Processed" (4), from *Once Removed* (Persea Books, 2015). Reprinted with permission.

Allen Braden, "Shakabrah Diner" (49), from *20/20: Tacoma in Images and Verse*, https://peterserko.com/20-20-tacoma-in-images-and-verse/. Reprinted with permission.

Gertrude Haley Bader, "Tacoma Rainbow" (60), from *The Poetry of Gertrude Haley Bader*, (Pageant Press, Inc., 1961). Reprinted with permission.

Elizabeth Bradfield, "Eagles Every Day" (159), from *Once Removed* (Persea Books, 2015). Reprinted with permission.